GLASTONBURY
MYTH & ARCHAEOLOGY

GLASTONBURY
MYTH & ARCHAEOLOGY

PHILIP RAHTZ
& LORNA WATTS

In memory of Stephen Morland and his 91 years at Glastonbury

Hence let us go, as in pilgrimage, to the famous Glastonbury;
for it is a very rough and disagreeable road, over rocks and the heads of rivers

William Stukeley, 1723

First published 1993
This edition first published 2009

The History Press
The Mill, Brimscombe Port
Stroud, Gloucestershire, gl 5 2QG
www.thehistorypress.co.uk

British Library Cataloguing in Publication Data.
A catalogue record for this book is available from the British Library.

ISBN 978 0 7524 5049 0

Typesetting and origination by The History Press
Printed in Great Britain

CONTENTS

ACKNOWLEDGEMENTS

Our indebtedness to many people and institutions extends back over more than thirty years, to the time when Rahtz was invited to dig at Chalice Well; this led to further excavation at Glastonbury Tor and Beckery, consolidating his interest in the early medieval period in this area. We would especially like to thank the late Stephen and Margot Morland, who were part of the Glastonbury scene for nearly the whole of the last century. They provided hospitality and encouragement throughout the excavations and the writing of this book; Stephen had read and corrected earlier drafts before his death in 1993. Nancy and Charles Hollinrake, now the 'resident archaeologists' of Glastonbury, have generously provided much detail of their numerous recent excavations and research. Warwick Rodwell and Christopher Hawkes have contributed much useful comment and material. James Carley and the late Ralegh Radford, who have both written extensively on Glastonbury, have provided comment on unpublished material, and illustrations. David Bromwich, Peter Leach, Mick Aston, James Bond, the Gloucester Record Office, and the British Museum have provided illustrations; Bob Croft and Stephen Minnitt have helped to update this version.

We would also thank the Trustees of the Abbey for their collaboration in work there, through the kind offices of Penny Cudmore, Prebendary Hodge and Commander Scadding.

The line drawings and photographs are by the authors, except for the following: **25**, **38** and **40** from Carley 1981, by kind permission; **19**, **20**, **46** and **47** from Sir Henry Spelman's *Concilia* (1639-64), by permission of the Society of Antiquaries; 4 by Gloucester Record Office; **49** by David Bromwich from the original published in the excavation report; **51** reproduced by courtesy of the Trustees of the British Museum (BM 210168 copyright); **75** and **76** by permission of the Somerset County Museums Service; and Mick Aston for **colour plate 1**. The cover picture is from Mick Sharpe. Other line figures are reproduced or redrawn from other published sources, as indicated on each drawing or caption.

Finally, we are indebted to the instigators of this book, English Heritage, Batsford and Tempus, through Stephen Johnson, Peter Kemmis Betty and Michelle Burns for their critical comment; and to Judith Dobie of English Heritage, who has graced this book with her splendid reconstructions. Beverley McJannett has typed the text, an exercise in decipherment of hieroglyphics.

In this revised edition Bob Croft would like to thank the Trustees of Glastonbury Abbey and Somerset County Museums Service for **colour plates 4**, **16–24**, **27, 28** and **29**, and Somerset Archaeological and Natural History Society for **colour plate 9**. Thanks are also due to Duncan Smart, Robert Dunning, Lawrence Bostock, Richard Brunning and Stephen Minnitt.

1

INTRODUCTION

Glastonbury is one of the best-known places in Britain, and a familiar name to millions of people in English-speaking areas of the world. It is indeed a place of the greatest historical importance, and is rich in archaeological evidence. This, however, while absorbing to academic historians and archaeologists, is not the reason for its popular fame, which depends on its legendary associations with the earliest Christianity in Britain; and on the massive accretion of its supposed association with King Arthur, Joseph of Arimathea and other well-known characters. Glastonbury's reputation has accelerated massively during the last century and especially in recent decades. It has become something of a magnet for idealistic visionaries, who see the place as having some intrinsic power apparently quite distinct from its history. To some it is comparable with Mecca or with the major pilgrimage centres of the Christian Church. Like Stonehenge, it has become a focus for migrations of young (and not so young) people, to the extent of posing a threat to the local environment.

Historically, Glastonbury is famous principally for its Abbey. From late Saxon times onwards, it was one of the richest, and at times the richest, of all the great Benedictine houses in England. Its monastic reputation was enhanced by royal patronage, including royal burials. In this book, the question is posed: why was the Abbey so famous? Was it because of the rich natural resources of the area, which are well-attested in earlier centuries and millennia? Or was its fame, instead, a result of its legendary associations with the earliest Christian missionaries; or of the brilliant exploitation of these legends and the concomitant attraction of political power? And what has all this to do with its present day reputation?

To write yet another book about Glastonbury may seem superfluous and even foolhardy. But so much of what has been written is of dubious value (to be polite). Myth and history are inextricably woven together, so that it is difficult for the discerning reader to find the truth; or rather, the closest approach to the truth that historical and archaeological scholarship is able to provide.

This is, it is hoped, not just another book to add to the strange miscellany on sale at the Abbey bookstall. Nor is it intended just as a guidebook to the town and its monuments. It seeks instead to present a balanced picture of past and present Glastonbury, from its prehistoric and Roman origins, through its fame as a great Saxon and medieval abbey to its final disastrous ruination at the hands of Henry VIII; and beyond to its present-day idiosyncratic status.

The material for this book is diverse in character. Historical sources are plentiful but discrete, in the sense that the further discovery of any major documents about Glastonbury is most unlikely. The archaeological potential, however, has hardly been tapped. The evidence still buried below the ground is extremely rich, and it is to be hoped that much of it will survive the ravages of modern development. The work undertaken so far has not, however, always been of the highest quality, not least because each decade sees such remarkable developments in archaeological method and application of scientific techniques. Ultimately, it may be hoped that archaeology will provide further answers to some of the problems posed in this book.

The first part of the book looks at the natural landscape and environment of the Glastonbury area, and the resources for human and economic development that these provide. The earliest archaeological evidence is then described. Just outside the limits of the town are the well-known lake or marsh settlements of the pre-Roman centuries; and beyond these, in the wetlands of the Somerset Levels, there is abundant evidence of human settlement and communication extending back to the fifth millennium BC. This prehistoric background, together with the evidence for Roman exploitation, is briefly surveyed. Little material of these earlier periods has been found in the Glastonbury peninsula itself, though what is known will be noted.

The story of Glastonbury as a Christian centre is next explored, firstly through its history. Here the discussion is restricted to what would nowadays be called a 'reductionist' or 'minimalist' summary of what are generally believed to be 'true' facts and interpretations. Secondly, the remarkable accretion of myth that has developed around Glastonbury is examined. The nature and reliability of this is still a matter of emotive debate, though much can be shown to have medieval origins.

The main part of the book is, however, concerned with archaeology. Excavations will be described and discussed: on the Tor, in the Abbey and its precinct, and at Chalice Well; and further afield, at the bank and ditch called Ponter's Ball, the earthwork known as the Mound, and the daughter monastery of Beckery. This part of the book is the first such overall exposition of material which is largely neglected or misunderstood in earlier books.

The history of the Abbey as an institution ended with the Dissolution and the savage execution of the last abbot on the Tor. The book concludes with a discussion of the gradual rise of the modern fame of the town, enhanced by drama, music and other cultural activities. Today Glastonbury is a flourishing modern town, beset by industry and tourism. Its historical monuments are, however, still a matter of great interest. We hope that this book will do something to stimulate interest in the appreciation of the true rather than the bogus Glastonbury. The facts about the place are exciting enough: they do not need embellishments or vulgar personalisation. Nevertheless, there is a present day clash of interests between those who would like to preserve and improve the appearance of the place and its historical importance, and those who seek to exploit it for commercial gain. To echo the problems associated with another very famous place in England, Stonehenge, one may ask: 'Whose Glastonbury is it?' And can these conflicting claims be resolved or reconciled?

2

WHY GLASTONBURY?
ENVIRONMENT AND RESOURCES

Land, Sea and Rain

The Isle of Apples, truly fortunate
Where enforc'd goods and willing comforts meet
Not there the fields require the rustic's hand
But Nature only cultivates the land
The fertile plains with corn and herbs are proud
And golden apples smile in ev'ry wood

William Camden, 1695

The Levels must have been either a gloomy waste of waters, or a still
more hideous expanse of reeds and other aquatic plants, impassable by
human foot, and involved in an atmosphere pregnant with pestilence
and death

Richard Warner, 1829

Geology and topography

Glastonbury is not an island, and has not been one in recent geological time. It is
a peninsula, linked to higher ground to the east by a neck of land nowhere lower
than 10m (33ft) above modern sea level (**1** & **colour plate 3**). To travellers from
the west, coming by water, it may have looked like an island, with water or watery
moors on three sides; the land link was invisible from this side.

The Glastonbury peninsula is based on strata of Lias beds of Jurassic age. The
lower beds are of a clayey limestone, laid down in layers (hence Lias) and very
convenient for quarrying building stone. Above these are less stable marlstones
and clays (**2**). All later geological layers have been removed by erosion, except
for a capping of hard Midford Sand on the summit of the Tor – this is sandstone,
which has largely resisted erosion (below, p.18). The instability of the lower beds
of the Tor have given rise to extensive defoliation (toppling out of hard lumps or
boulders, known as Tor Burrs), fragmentation and fissuring; the latter was vividly

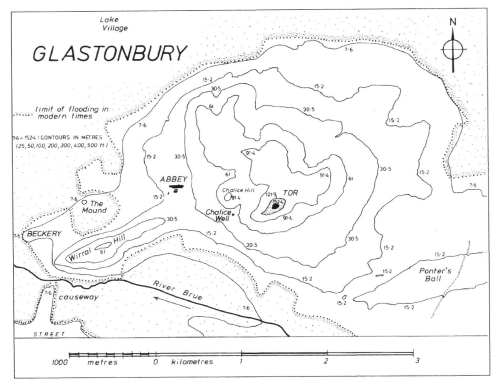

1 *Contours of the Glastonbury peninsula; note the location of Ponter's Ball across the higher 'neck' to the east.* PAR, 1992

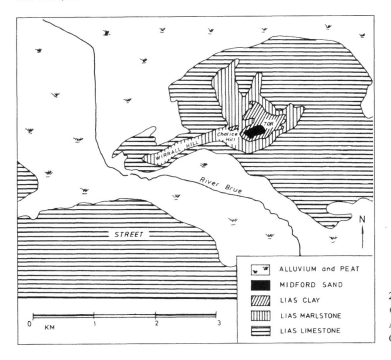

2 *The geology of the Glastonbury/Street area.* After Dale and Gannaway, 1960

encountered in the excavations there (p.69). Erosion of the peninsula has taken place not only over long periods of geological time but more recently, with the carving out of river valleys in the area, notably the Brue and its tributaries (see **4**), to a depth of several metres.

The relationship between land and sea levels has also been variable. At times, the river valleys, with their changing courses, would have been dry land. But when the sea levels were relatively higher (the sea level rising or the land-mass dropping), the whole of the lower areas could be inundated; estuarine marine sediments have been identified close to Glastonbury, dating to the first millennium BC.

There has been considerable debate (often heated) about the chronology and extent of such inundations ('marine transgressions') (**3**) of the lower areas, or the Somerset Levels as we may now call them. It is, however, generally agreed that there was severe flooding in the second to first millennia BC and again in the early medieval period, the latter after a drier phase in Roman times. The problem is to discover how much variation in the extent of flooding is related to dune formation, and how much is due to Roman and later attempts to 'hold back' the sea by seawalls, floodbanks and other forms of water control; evidence of inundation can at times be interpreted in this scenario as the result of neglect of such works.

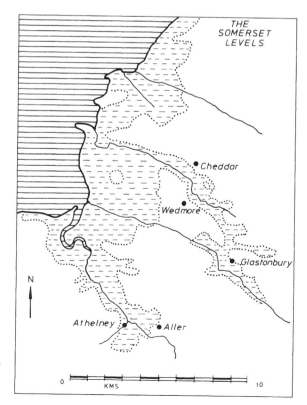

3 *The extent of marine flooding in the early medieval period; this, and the dating, are still matters of debate.*
After Hill, 1981

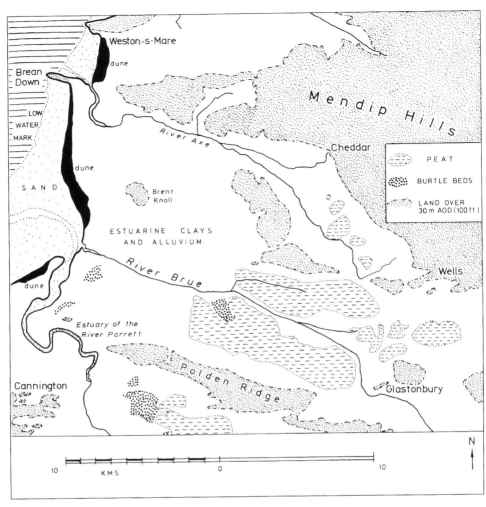

4 *The topography of the area between Glastonbury and the Bristol Channel; note the 'islands' of the harder Burtle Beds, and the extent to which dune formation helps to prevent flooding from the sea.* After Bell, 1990

It is only in recent times that the sea has been brought (temporarily) under control by very extensive seawalls, and the cutting of water channels ('rhynes' or 'cuts'), for the greater control of both salt and fresh water. It is, however, not only the sea which has caused flooding, but also rain. In times of heavy falls (up to 20cm (8in)) on Mendip and other neighbouring hills, the rivers burst their banks, and the aspect looks decidedly marine (**colour plate 2**); there is insufficient gradient to carry the water out to sea.

Combined marine and freshwater flooding has raised the ground level to some extent by the deposition of silts, the alluvium which extends around the Glastonbury peninsula and right through the Levels to the sea. On much of this, beds of peat have developed, up to 7m (23ft) deep (**4**).

There are thus two landscapes: firstly the visible peninsula itself with 'islands' in the Levels, some of Lias and some of harder Burtle Beds (**4**), ancient marine sand deposits where the archaeological remains are relatively shallow beneath present turf and topsoil; and secondly a vast buried landscape, where roadways, settlements and other features are deeply sealed by alluvium and peat. Glastonbury was open and exposed to the west, the flat aspect broken only by the humps of Brent Knoll and Brean Down. It could be reached from this direction by water: either directly at times of the greatest inundation, or by way of the rivers. These would also be deeper (allowing navigation by larger boats) at times of relatively high sea level (chapter 9).

Floods may have allowed access, but they were also a problem – the gravity of which is witnessed by the extent of the successive works that have been and are being undertaken to control them. Local histories are eloquent on the suffering caused. On 20 January 1606:

> the sea, at a flowing water, meeting with land floods, strove so violently together that heaving down all things it was builded to withstand and hinder the force of them, the banks were eaten through, and a rupture was made into Somersetshire.

The whole of the Brue Levels were flooded 3-4m (10-13ft) deep; ricks floated away, 'but the company of Hogs and Pigs went on eating on top . . . rabbits on sheeps' backs were drowned with them'. Floodwater extended up to St John's Church in Glastonbury, with water 2m (over 6ft) deep in the streets. The same thing happened in 1703. Babies were drowned in their cradles of willow bark; this led to the invention of cradles with raised joists to keep them above the water.

The variety of terrain around these two contrasting landscapes is still striking. To the south-west are the Polden Hills; and to the north the great mass of Mendip, rising to over 320m (1,050ft), and dominating the northern skyline. The routes by which materials, and people, were carried from these areas will be considered further in chapter 9.

The basic rock-forms, their accumulation, erosion and distortion, are responsible for the main shapes of the landscape, water from the sky and sea contributing their own forces. Wetlands and drylands, with their varying soil types, provide the basic environment for plant growth, which in turn affords shelter and food for a wide range of life-forms, including humans. It is against this natural background that we must view the remarkable sequence of events that comprise the history of Glastonbury, and the exploitation of its resources.

Resources

Early humans, in remote prehistory, would, like the animals, have developed life-styles appropriate to the terrain over which they ranged. As time passed, humans not only took from the environment, but altered it, progressively creating the Glastonbury of today. The basic landscape remains, however, largely unchanged, if viewed on a misty day from the Levels or from the top of Mendips, the Tor still remains a major and dramatic landmark, with the tiny pencil-like church tower at the peak.

The resources available to the inhabitants of Glastonbury and its vicinity (whether they were the earlier Neolithic farming communities or medieval peasants) comprised not only the rich yields from the Levels and coast, but also those from the surrounding uplands. How much use could be made of these depended on the ease of exchange and trade between neighbouring groups, or the degree of coercion that could be brought to bear by war-leaders or abbots.

It must not be imagined that (especially in prehistoric times) all communities were permanently settled in one place. As will be seen in the case of the so-called 'Lake Villages', there is reason to believe that many sites were occupied only seasonally, the Levels in the summer, the uplands (and caves) in the winter. The year was a seasonal round, dependent on weather and the level of the water table. Each week or month had its own tasks; this agricultural cycle is summarised in **5**, and is splendidly illustrated in medieval psalters and other works. From earliest prehistory, humans exchanged goods and produce with other humans, thus enlarging the variety that was available from the local resources of upland and marsh. By the end of the first millennium BC, such exchange mechanisms had extended as far as the Mediterranean; in later centuries to the whole world.

It will be useful to survey firstly the resources that were available locally, and secondly the ways in which these were extended. While discussion on 'natural' resources is especially appropriate to prehistoric Glastonbury, these still dominated the economy of the medieval abbey. Archaeologically, there is a remarkable range of evidence provided by excavations in the Levels to the west of the town, which have been in progress for most of the twentieth century. The richness of these areas is due to the extent of preservation afforded by ground that has been waterlogged for at least seven millennia. Here archaeology is indebted to four people who have recovered this evidence and analysed it – Arthur Bulleid and Harold St George Gray in the earlier decades of the twentieth century, and John and Bryony Coles in recent decades. The Coles have been responsible for one of the most successful archaeological research projects ever undertaken in Britain. It is now of international repute, as an example of collaboration between archaeologists and a wide variety of scientists.

On the drier areas of Glastonbury there have also been very extensive excavations during most of the twentieth century: environmental evidence from these is, however, minimal compared to that recovered from the Levels, the most useful being the animal bones (food residues) which do survive.

Complementary to the archaeological evidence for the range of resources and their exploitation, there are the historical sources: the details in medieval documents on the management of the Glastonbury Abbey estates. Although these extend to cover a much wider catchment area than the local upland and marsh, they provide the same kind of evidence. The basic economy of the marsh edges in prehistory is summarised in **6**. To these resources can be added other items available at a slightly greater distance, some of them exploited only in Roman and later times. The Mendip Hills yielded lead, silver and other minerals. In Saxon times this was a royal forest, a favourite venue for aristocratic hunting (p.43). Some areas could be emparked for deer: the Abbey had ultimately no less than seven deer parks.

While the watery moors provided a wide variety of fish, fowl and mammals (including otter and beaver), expeditions to the Bristol Channel or contact with traders extended the range of food stuffs to salt, sea-fish, sea-fowl and molluscs. Locally, the Meare Pool (**83**) was a very useful reservoir for fish. In medieval times, fish and eels were both farmed by the construction of special installations and water control systems. Pigs and other animals were pastured in the Levels and reeds

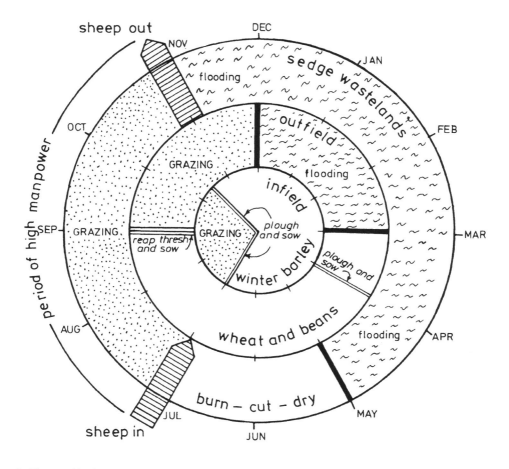

5 *The use of land in the Levels throughout the year; note the seasonal incidence of flooding.* After Clarke 1972

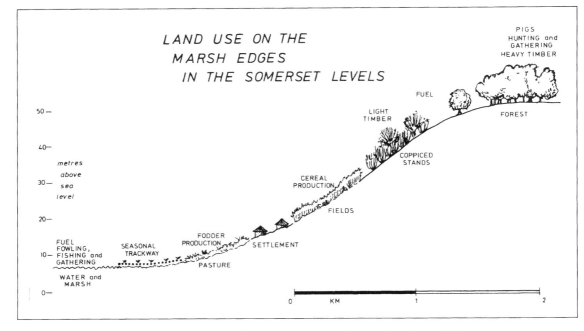

6 *The diverse resources of the Levels and the higher ground around them.* After Coles, 1982

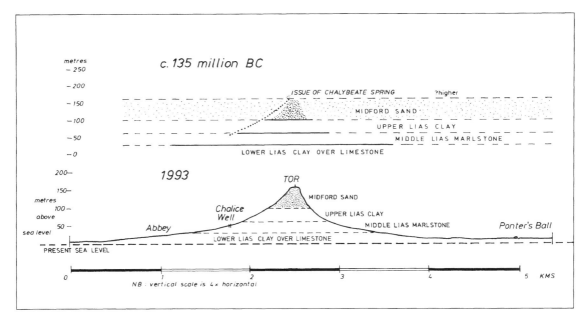

7 *The origins of the Tor. The Midford Sand which comprises the upper part of the Tor is the residue of much more extensive deposits; it is suggested that the reason for this surviving fragment is that it was anciently hardened by iron compounds from the spring which now feeds Chalice Well; as the clayey deposits were eroded away, the spring steadily dropped to its present level.* After PAR, 1992

were used for lights. Extensive use was made of the water channels for transport (see chapter 9).

The effectiveness of the water systems in medieval times depended on both the maintenance of seawalls and sluices to contain sea water at high tide; and on the management, by embanking, cleaning and revetment, of channels and fishponds. When dykes and walls had been broken down in the early fourteenth century, for example, it was complained that 'the water poured in and drowned 1,000 acres of corn, barley, beans, pease and oats; also 50 acres of meadowland and 300 acres of pasture . . . the land remained drowned for 2 years and things have gone from bad to worse. . .'. The Somerset Levels, however, when conserved, were an important economic asset not only to the abbots of Glastonbury but also to the bishops of Wells. There are numerous accounts of rivalry between them, resulting in legal wrangles, and, worse, to open warfare, with attacks on drainage operations and fish farms, with swords and bows, used from boats.

The rivers, at least in earlier centuries, provided not only routes for boats, but also plentiful water for washing and drinking. There were major springs on the peninsula itself, the most important being that rising from Chalice Well (p.134). Water also allowed the creation of canals (p.146) and provided, in medieval times (if not earlier), the power for watermills. These were supplemented, after the twelfth century, by windmills (see chapter 9).

Another useful natural product that eventually came under human control was honey. This provided in early times not only the main sweetening agent (before the import of sugar), but also the principal medium with which to make alcohol, in the form of mead; this figures very largely in Anglo-Saxon and medieval documents. Thus in 1262, an annual payment of '4 gallons of honey to the Glastonbury medary annually' is referred to. Wax was used for altar candles, which could weigh several pounds.

Finally, especially in Roman times and later, there was an abundance of clay for making pottery, ovens, bricks and tiles, and a very easily-worked stone, the tabular Lias limestone. The beds of the latter at Street were especially suitable and much quarried. This stone was used for basic building, but was not suitable for carving door or window members, or sculpture. For this, recourse was had to the oolitic limestones outside the immediate area, at Bath, Ham Hill, Dundry and Doulting. At the latter place, the Abbey had a large quarry; this stone was in extensive use in the area from the tenth century onwards.

More exotic materials would be sought from further afield, and some will be referred to in later pages, such as shale and pottery from Dorset, and Purbeck limestone from the same area. The most remarkable finds, however, are of Mediterranean origin: sixth-century amphorae, the large pottery vessels used to transport many commodities. Sherds of these have been found at two of the sites excavated in the peninsula (the Tor and the Mound) (pp.69, 138); from this distant area also came a seventh-century leaded brass censer found near the Abbey (**68**).

Some aspects of the ancient economy have been especially persistent into modern times. Glastonbury and Street are well-known for sheepskin and leather shoes and other products, reflecting the extensive local grazing areas. The willow of the Levels is still used for basket- and hurdle-making, though decreasingly. It is, however, peat which has dominated the area. It was formerly, from prehistoric times down to the middle of the twentieth century, cut by hand and stacked up to dry for home fuel. It has been a major industry, the peat-beds being removed by huge mechanical vehicles for agricultural fertilizer. This has posed a major threat both to the archaeology and to the environment.

This chapter will conclude by proposing an answer to the question in its title – why Glastonbury? It is suggested that humans were impressed by the remarkable form of the Tor, rising from its peninsula. It is a striking landmark, especially as seen from the Levels, comparable to the appearance of Mount Ararat in Turkey, towering above the flat plains which surround it. The Tor is visible from the greater part of central Somerset, from distances of up to 40km (25 miles) (see **25** and chapter 6).

Its shape was established a very long time before humans ever saw it or found it impressive. The cause was the isolated cap of Midford Sand of only a few hundred square metres which resisted erosion and was left proud when all surrounding strata were removed by natural agency. It can be suggested that the reason for its survival was the consolidation caused by the iron-rich spring which now rises from Chalice Well (**7**). The source of this has gradually dropped to its present location lower down, as the strata from which it issued were removed. The seeds of Glastonbury's fame were thus sown some 135 million years ago, in the age of the dinosaurs.

3

PREHISTORIC AND ROMAN GLASTONBURY

In this chapter, the prehistoric and Roman background of the Glastonbury area is summarised. There is as yet little evidence of either in the peninsula itself, but this negative evidence is of importance in assessing subsequent developments in the post-Roman centuries. In contrast, there is massive archaeological evidence from the nearby Somerset Levels and this must be considered along with the peninsula because, as has been noted, the wetlands are a fundamental part of the economic resources of the area.

The earliest settlers

The earliest possible evidence for human settlement in the area is from about half a million years ago. This consists of flints found in a quarry fissure at Westbury-sub-Mendip, a few kilometres west of Wells; very numerous fossilised bones of extinct animals were also found. Unfortunately, the flints are not very distinctive, and there is some doubt as to whether they are of human manufacture or not.

Palaeolithic flint and chert implements (dating to 75,000 BC and later) of more recognisable types have been found with the bones of extinct animals in other fissures, and in caves such as Hyaena Den, close to Wookey Hole, again just west of Wells; there were also hearths suggesting human use.

With an improvement in the climate from about 15,000 BC, more frequent indications of human settlement, by *Homo sapiens sapiens* (modern man) have been found. Open sites are unlikely to be discovered because of their vulnerability to erosion, but there are well-preserved deposits in the caves of the Mendips, to the north of Glastonbury – at Cheddar and at Burrington. Here there are implements and tools of flint and other stone, and bone; and also the earliest human remains from the area: 'Cheddar Man' – a young adult skeleton from Gough's Cave, and over 50 skeletons from Aveline's Hole at Burrington. The latter seems to have been a 'burial cave'; there may even have been objects buried with the humans – perforated animal teeth, winkle shells and fossil ammonites. The dates of the skeletons at both Cheddar and Burrington are around 11,000 BC.

At these cave sites, something can be said of the local climate and landscape from the kinds of animals represented by the remains. There is also pollen, of abundant birch and willow, with grass and sedge from damper areas. By about 9000 BC the tundra-like conditions were giving way to deciduous woodland.

It may be imagined that these earliest Somerset humans would have made use of the open areas south of Mendip, exploiting what they could of the resources described in the previous chapter. Such activity by hunter-gatherer groups (if not actual settlement) is well represented by flints (microliths) and stone tools of distinctive types. Many of these have been found in the Somerset Levels near Glastonbury, notably on the 'islands' which rise above the wetlands. A few flints which may be of this period were found in the excavations at Chalice Well, on the peninsula itself (p.134); this great spring was doubtless an attractive focus of visitation, if not of settlement.

It was during this period that the river valleys of the Levels were colonised by reeds and willow scrub, providing ample fodder for larger mammals (wild cattle, deer, pigs and horses). Pike and migratory salmon would have provided other food; and the pools and reeds gave shelter to numerous wildfowl. Conditions for both fish and fowl may have been assisted by the dam-building activities of beavers. Differences in the flint assemblages suggest seasonal activities by groups ranging widely over both the Levels and the surrounding upland areas.

Farmers and their trackways (4000–2000 BC)

The first definite evidence of settled occupation of the Glastonbury area belongs to the Neolithic period. Pits and hearths were found in excavations at the hilltop of South Cadbury, to the south of Glastonbury (**8**); associated with them were flint (leaf-shaped) arrowheads, pottery, ox bones, deer antler, hazelnuts and human bones. At Wells, pits were also found in the Cathedral excavations, with leaf-shaped arrowheads and pottery. There have also been finds from the Mendip caves, including Cheddar.

Outside the area, religious monuments (stone circles and henges) are known in the north of the county (Stanton Drew) and on Mendip (Priddy Circles and Gorsey Bigbury); here, there are also numerous long barrows (communal burial mounds).

One of the dominant activities of the first farmers in the region was the clearance of the land of tree and scrub. This was assisted by the perfection achieved in the technology of the ground and polished stone axe, hafted with wood and antler. These axes are often of flint, imported from the chalklands to east and south; but many were of stone, from areas as distant as Cornwall, Brittany and Cumbria. There is continuing debate about the extent to which these were the products of 'axe-factories', specialised centres of production of finished tools or rough-outs; or whether they resulted from the collection of glacial erratics from these areas. Over 200 such axes have been found in Somerset; nearly half are made of stone from distant areas.

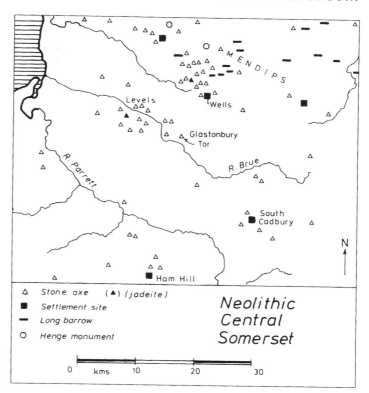

8 *The distribution of Neolithic stone axes, settlements and religious monuments around Glastonbury.* After Norman 1982

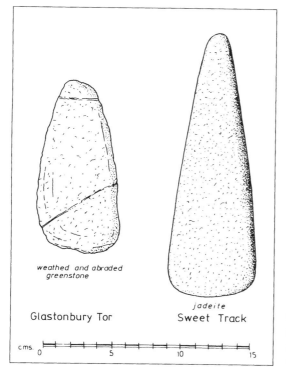

9 *Neolithic axes; the jadeite example (right) has not been used, and is likely to have been a votive offering; it is made of a rock found only in Brittany.* PAR, 1992

The distribution of these axes around Glastonbury is shown in **8**. It will be seen that most were found in the Levels, but one was found on Glastonbury Tor (**9**) with other flint tools. The possibility that the Tor itself was fashioned into a great Neolithic ceremonial monument − a maze − may seem to border on the lunatic fringe, but the possibility is at least discussed in chapter 6.

The most remarkable structures of the Neolithic and later centuries are, however, the wooden trackways which crossed the Levels in many places, linking areas of higher ground (**10**). These have survived remarkably well in the water-logged ground, but are now in danger of drying out due to the effects of modern commercial peat-cutting. It is, at the same time, this activity which has revealed them, together with a mass of environmental data (including pollen and beetles) and artefacts (arrows, metal tools, dug-out boats etc.). The existence of such tracks has been known for nearly two centuries. In 1835 one was named the Abbot's Way, because it was thought to be the work of monks. It is now dated to about 2500 BC!

The trackways were made of planks, poles or rails, secured by pegs or other timbers. The oldest is the Sweet Track, discovered in 1970. This is made of ash, oak and hazel, with pegs of hazel, holly, alder, ash and elm; the whole is packed with peat. Thanks to the precision now made possible by tree-ring dating, exact dates can be given for this and other trackways. The Sweet Track is dated to the winter of 3807-3806 BC; it was thus nearly 6,000 years old. The evidence shows that it was all constructed in one operation. The timber (4,000m (13,000ft) of plank, 2,000m

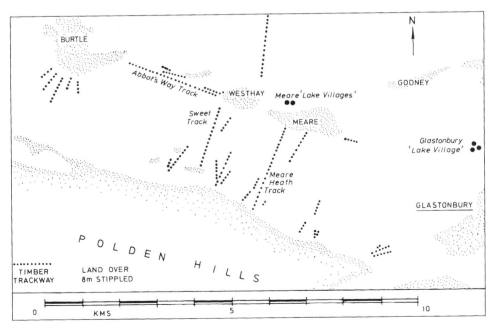

10 *Prehistoric settlements and trackways west of Glastonbury; the trackways are of different dates and have been found at different levels in the peat. After Coles, 1982*

(6,500ft) of heavy rails and 6,000 pegs) had to be felled, split and prepared before being carried to both ends of a line 1,800m (6,000ft) long. It is estimated that the whole track could then have been completed by ten people in a few days in the spring of 3806 BC.

The track was built to be used at a time of increasing flooding. Its life was no more than ten years, before it was overwhelmed by water and reeds. It then became useless, firstly in winter, and then in summer. The exact dating thus applies not only to the track itself, but to the use of a wide range of finds associated with it. The magnitude of work suggests that there was an organised community in the area with considerable resources of manpower.

The artefacts that are so well-dated were found along the entire length. They include broken pots (one full of hazelnuts, another with a wooden stirring spoon); wooden tools; flint knives and arrowheads; polished yew pins (for hair or nose?); a long-bow of yew (**11**); and stone axes. Two of the latter, one of jadeite from Brittany (see **9**) and one of flint, had never been used; they are thought to have been votive offerings, as was a carved wooden figurine. Later trackways were of various kinds of construction. The Meare Heath Track, of the second millennium BC, is shown in **11**; others used prepared hurdles. The latter are evidence for controlled coppicing from *c.*3000 BC, a technique surviving to modern times.

Some trackways converge at platforms, the edges of the raised areas. One at Westhay may have also served as a landing for canoes or rafts; preserved dung beetles showed cattle were being driven across the trackways.

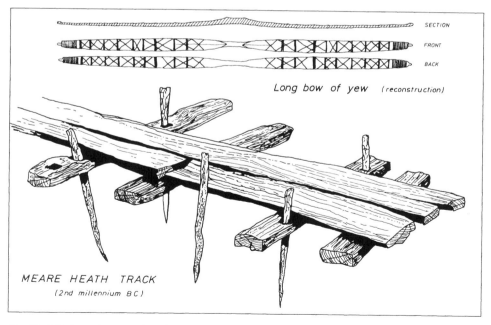

11 *Neolithic bow of yew-wood, and detail of the construction of the Meare Heath trackway, of rails and long pointed pegs.* After Coles 1982

The Bronze and Iron Ages

It is to the third and second centuries BC that the open settlements, which have made Glastonbury one of the best-known names in archaeology, belong. These are the 'Lake Villages' of Glastonbury and Meare. They were not, however, in a lake, nor were they permanent villages in the medieval sense; a better name would be marsh-edge settlements, more probably of only seasonal use.

The one near Glastonbury was discovered a century ago, in 1892, by Arthur Bulleid. He had read of piled lake-dwellings in Switzerland, and looked for similar structures on the moors; digging into low mounds, he discovered many finds of wooden structures, and with H. St George Gray, excavated the settlements in the first half of the twentieth century. The settlement at Glastonbury was built in an area of the Levels where open water predominated. It was built on a great platform of felled timber, in a similar fashion to the crannogs, built in lakes, which are numerous in Ireland and Scotland. This sub-structure incorporated a landing stage and palisade, inside which were many buildings. These were circular, with a thick clay floor, vertical wattle and daub walls, and a raised hearth.

Analysis of Bulleid and Gray's excavation reports by the late David Clarke is one of the classic studies in modern British archaeology. Taking into account the stratigraphy and the distribution of artefacts, structures of many different types and the postulated phases of growth, Clarke suggested there were areas of specialised activities and structures occupied only by women. His theoretical reconstruction of the settlement at its maximum extent is shown in **12**.

In the 1990s the evidence relating to Glastonbury Lake Village was subjected to a thorough re-evaluation, using Bullied and Gray's excavation achives together with the results of more recent research. This work shed considerable light on the environmental setting, the development of the site over time and some of the on-site activities (Coles and Minnitt 1995). One important outcome was to demonstrate that David Clarke's 'classic study' of the site was theoretical only.

Studies by Rupert Housley and others have shown that the settlement was located in a swamp comprising areas of standing water, reed beds, sedge fen and patched of fen carr. One of these areas of fen carr was selected for the site of the settlement. The trees, willow and alder, were felled and supplemented by logs, stone and brushwood from the nearby dry land to create the beginnings of an artificial island which was to be expanded over time. Clay spreads were deposited on the island, some served as the floors of round houses, others as the bases for industrial and other outdoor activities, sheds and animal pens. Hundreds of tonnes of clay, stone and timber and other raw materials were imported over the 150 years or so of the settlement's existence. Travel to from the site would have been by log boat or raft, the nearest dry land was 1.5km away. A landing stage projected out into the standing water to the east.

Throughout its existence the settlement underwent constant change — new buildings, repairs, modifications, demolition and accidental destruction by fire,

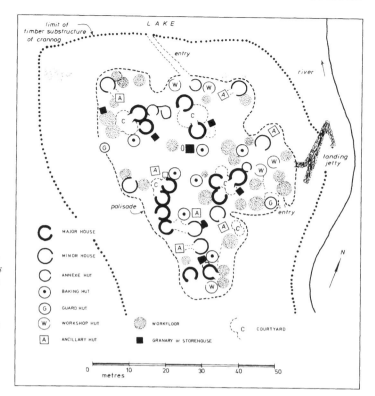

12 *The plan of the Glastonbury Lake Village. The function of the various buildings was suggested by the late David Clarke on the basis of an exhaustive analysis of the field records of Bulleid and Gray; not everyone agrees with his interpretation.*
After Clarke 1972

sometimes areas were abandoned or their use changed. From small beginnings in about 200 BC, when there were perhaps five or six houses, the island was gradually expanded to an area of one hectare and provided a base for a maximum of perhaps 15 houses and a population of maybe 200 people. The enormous quantities of artefacts provide an exceptional insight into domestic life and craft and small-scale industrial activities in the later Iron Age. A timber palisade surrounded the settlement, perhaps in part for reasons of defence but it also served as a structural function helping prevent the settlement from spreading and sinking – there was an enormous weight upon a soft peat base.

All the evidence points to Glastonbury Lake Village having been permanently occupied. That is, until the middle decades of the first century BC when the site underwent a profound change, it diminished in size and the population reduced in number. The cause was gradually rising water levels from which there was no protection in such a location. Occupation may well have become seasonal at this stage. Life on the site soon became untenable and it was abandoned in about 50 BC.

These settlements provide a striking contrast with other types of Iron Age site, notably the hillforts such as Compton Dundon and South Cadbury, lying some distance to the south of Glastonbury. What has not been found is the burial-place of the marsh settlers. Bulleid offered a substantial reward for information which would lead to their discovery; but this was never claimed.

It has often been suggested, romantically, that the Glastonbury peninsula, the 'Isle of Avalon', was where they should be. Little of this date has been found, however, just a few Iron Age sherds at the Mound, at Chalice Well and at Beckery, implying at least frequentation. Yet there remains a possibility that the whole peninsula could be a very large Iron Age 'territory', of either a secular or religious nature; the reason for this suggestion is an earthwork at the east end, which may now be considered in some detail.

Ponter's Ball

> This is the site of *Pontis Vallum*, the Fort of the Bridge, which defended
> the Isle of Avalon from the mainland. It was later called Ponter's Ball.

So runs the inscription on the metal plaque which lies half-hidden by shrub beside the road from Glastonbury to Shepton Mallet where this passes through the earthwork at Havyatt. Alternative variants are 'Ponting's Ball' (early nineteenth century) and 'Fonter's Ball' (1876); and it is also referred to (1923) as crossing Arthur's Causeway, a route which goes 'from Camelot to Avalon'. The name might be a local surname or might indeed be from *pontis* (bridge); 'ball' can mean a knoll or rounded hill. A further name has recently been suggested 'Portarius'. This family were the hereditary porters of the Abbey in the thirteenth century, and owned land in the vicinity of Havyatt.

The earthwork as seen today consists of a substantial bank, up to 10m (33ft) wide and 3.5m (11ft) high, with residues of a ditch on its east side (**13**). It extends for just over 1,000m (1,100yds) across a neck of slightly higher ground; this is the only natural entry to the Glastonbury peninsula which avoids the marshy area (the Street and other entry causeways are modern). From either side of the

13 *Ponter's Ball earthwork from the north; the ditch is on the left (east side)*

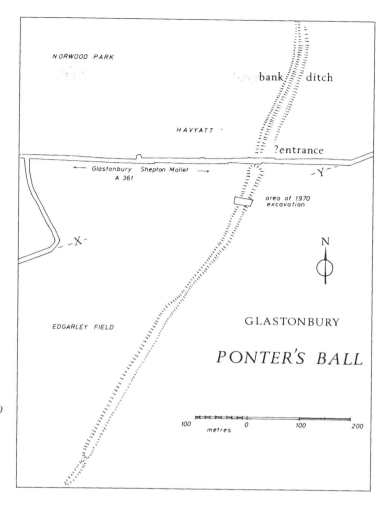

14 *The extent of Ponter's Ball; the 1970 excavation may have been on the site of an older road extending from X to Y. After C. Hollinrake, 1986*

present A361, the bank traverses this ridge before dropping away to the 10m (33ft) contour which indicates the approximate extent of former periodic flooding. The highest part of the bank is that immediately to the north and south of the road; but it is possible that it has been added to here by clearing or widening of the carriageway, or just possibly (see below) by making a cut through the earthwork where none had existed before. This would imply that the present course of the road is not the ancient route out of Glastonbury to the east.

The stretch to the south of the road is heavily disturbed; this was formerly part of the open fields of Glastonbury (Edgarley Field). To the north, in the deer park of Norwood, the earthwork is in a better state of preservation. From the present road, water would have drained down to the ditch to either end, there being a drop of up to 17m (55ft) in ground level. The earthwork may originally have extended further; if it does extend into the marshy area there would be a good chance of environmental or dating evidence being preserved.

The first excavation was undertaken in 1909 by Arthur Bulleid of Lake Village fame; he made a section north of the road. Prehistoric pottery, possibly Bronze Age, was found below the bank; and Iron Age pottery (of Lake Village type) was found deep in the ditch. The only other recorded excavation was in 1970. Partial sections were cut, 1.5m (5ft) wide in an area south of the road. The ditch was 2-3m (6-10ft) deep, and it is likely that the bank was at least as high as this, perhaps with some timber palisade or revetment. The western profile suggests a sharper internal bank.

Medieval and later pottery was found, with bone, below the turf on the west side. More significantly pottery was found in the original ground surface below the crest of the bank. This included Iron Age sherds from a shouldered urn (perhaps this was what Bulleid found below the bank); but there were also 15 late Saxon or medieval sherds. These could be matched with pottery from Cheddar Palace, Glastonbury Tor and Beckery; the date range was the tenth to twelfth centuries AD.

The bank, at the place examined at least, was thus of early medieval or later date. This was surprising, though it may be that this part is anomalous or disturbed. One possibility is that the area examined was formerly the route of another road or lane. It will be seen on **14** that there is a change of angle in the A361 just east of the earthwork and this formerly may have been a 'Y' junction, a lane leading off at Y, and extending south-west to join another lane at X; the latter winds back into Edgarley further west. A medieval or later date for the earthwork must be seriously considered, especially since the recorded stratification shows every appearance of a newly-constructed bank, using fresh material from the ditch, rather than dumped material put in to fill up a disused roadway or gap; but at present the earthwork as a whole must be considered as undated.

In a prehistoric, Iron Age context, the earthwork could be a cross-ridge dyke, defending a *territorium* of the Glastonbury peninsula or a wider area. There is a similar bank and ditch known as New Ditch 5km (3 miles) south (**15**), possibly cutting off the Polden Ridge, in the same way as Ponter's Ball does the Glastonbury peninsula. Bulleid found Iron Age pottery here too. Both earthworks may have had a similar function, and indeed may be part of one system associated with Glastonbury and its nearest hillfort at Compton Dundon; further fieldwork is needed here.

An alternative function for the earthwork in the Iron Age has also been put forward: that it was the eastern boundary of a great Celtic sanctuary around the Tor. If this were true it would do much to elucidate the origins of Glastonbury as a religious focus, and would perhaps lend more credence to the 'maze' theory (p.69).

Again (leaving aside the medieval sherds) it must be pointed out that the Iron Age pottery fragments provide only a date after which the earthwork was built – it could be Roman, Dark Age or Anglo-Saxon. The second of these must be a possibility in view of the Dark Age settlement on the Tor, especially if this is seen as a chieftain's stronghold (p.67). Such earthworks are characteristic of this period, acting as defences or boundary markers of Dark Age territories as they had in the Iron Age. In a local context, Wansdyke to the north can be cited. This is often interpreted as a defensive line facing rival powers north of the Avon, built by the men of Somerset in the period after their defeat at the Battle of Dyrham in 577.

Ponter's Ball could be part of a system fronting Anglo-Saxons to the east in the sixth century, or even a specific defence of the territorium of the 'king' on the Tor. It may be noted that the 'boundary' between Saxons and British in the sixth and seventh centuries, before the British defeat at Penselwood in 658, may have been approximately on the line of the Fosse Way (see **15**); pagan Anglo-Saxon cemeteries are entirely to the east of here. There is also the possibility of Ponter's Ball being the outer boundary of the great monastic 'city' of the Saxon centuries – an outer *vallum monasterii* (p.118).

Finally, is a medieval date, in or after *c*.1100, an historical possibility? The earthwork can hardly have been defensive at this time, but might have served as a land boundary defining the limits of some area regarded by the Abbey as sacrosanct, to which entry of visitors must be controlled, perhaps in order to pay a toll, as pilgrims or traders. Or were the bank and ditch so large to impress travellers with the great prestige of the Abbey and its twelfth-century Abbot (p.45)? The date and function of Ponter's Ball are thus very much an open question, to be answered only by further fieldwork and excavations.

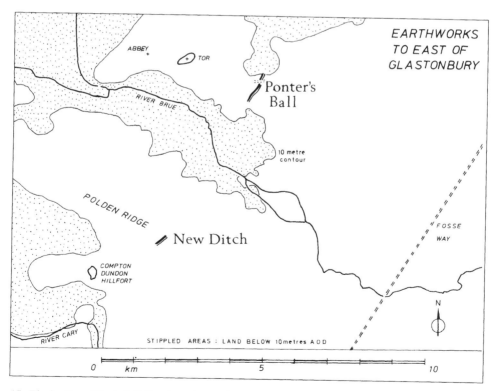

15 *The location of Ponter's Ball and another similar earthwork (New Ditch), extending across the crest of the Polden ridge. Such barriers are common in both prehistoric and Dark Age times.* After C. Hollinrake

Roman Glastonbury

Roman control of the area was established soon after the conquest by the Emperor Claudius, in AD 43. Especially valuable to the new masters were the lead and silver ores of Mendip (Charterhouse). These were used both in Britain (for instance for the lining of the great bath at Bath) and exported to Italy. Somerset (**16**) was never, however, of as much importance as other areas to the north and east; it remained predominantly as it had been, a mainly rural area, though the hillforts ceased to be of any significance.

A main route was established south-west to north-east from Exeter to Lincoln (the Fosse Way); this traverses the area just east of Glastonbury. On its route was the great religious baths/temple complex of *Aquae Sulis* (Bath); and roadside settlements at Camerton, Shepton Mallet and Ilchester (*Lindinis*). There were also small 'port' settlements in the estuary of the River Parrett, at Combwich and Crandon Bridge (**17**). These were reached from the Glastonbury area by way of a branch road down the ridge of the Polden Hills. Around Ilchester and Bath, villas developed as both rich dwellings and as controlling centres for agricultural and mineral production. There were also many pagan temples; the nearest one to Glastonbury (though unexcavated) is at Priest's Hill, Pedwell (**16**).

Glastonbury itself has, however, little evidence of any substantial Roman use. The name Street, and the route into Glastonbury via the causeway and on to Wells (p.141), may imply that this way was ancient and possibly of Roman origin. Roman sherds have been found at all the sites excavated in Glastonbury, but not in any quantity. Building materials (tiles etc.) suggest the existence of some structures in the Abbey area, and on the south slopes of Wirral Hill. There are also two wells in the Abbey, either or both of which may be Roman (one in the North Transept and that in the crypt of the Lady Chapel, p.106). There could also be important structures in the Abbey area which have so far eluded discovery. It will be suggested below (p.109) that the crypt well, if Roman, could (with its spring) be the nucleus of the use of that area, earlier than the building of the *vetusta ecclesia*, the oldest documented church at Glastonbury (p.61). To put this into perspective, before the archaeology of the Tor and the Abbey is examined in detail, the background of the origins of Christianity in Somerset and of the pagan religions which the new faith encountered, should be considered.

Pagan and Christian Somerset

As has been noted above, temples to the classical pagan deities abound in the area. The only dedication known for certain is that to Minerva at Bath, linked with the pre-Roman deity Sul; and Apollo has been suggested for the octagonal temple at Pagans Hill, north of Mendip.

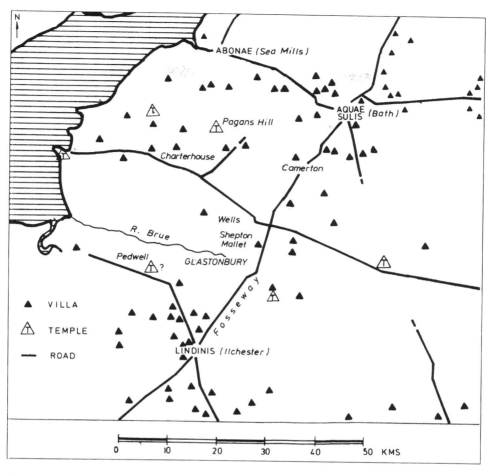

16 *Roman roads and sites around Glastonbury. The road system centres on the two towns of* Aquae Sulis *(Bath) and* Lindinis *(Ilchester); and provides links to coastal ports in the Bristol Channel*

Evidence for Roman Christianity in Somerset is, however, sparse (**17**). There are a few finds with Christian symbols, at Wint Hill and Gatcombe. The most important Christian find is a recent discovery, not far from Glastonbury. This is a round silver pendant, in the form of a cross; on one side is a punched dotted outline of a CHI-RHO monogram (C-R: *Christus Rex*), the symbol adopted by Constantine the Great and later emperors; it is dated to the late fourth or fifth century AD. The pendant was found in a grave, below the pelvis of a male skeleton. The grave was one of a number in a small enclosed cemetery set among buildings of the roadside settlement at Shepton Mallet, by the Fosse Way; the whole cemetery may be Christian (Leach, 2001).

Excavations at Wells Cathedral also have traced the sequence there back to an apparently late Roman date. The earliest structure was a stone-built mausoleum; this became the focus for a series of buildings which developed into the Saxon cathedral – so there may have been a Roman nucleus here too.

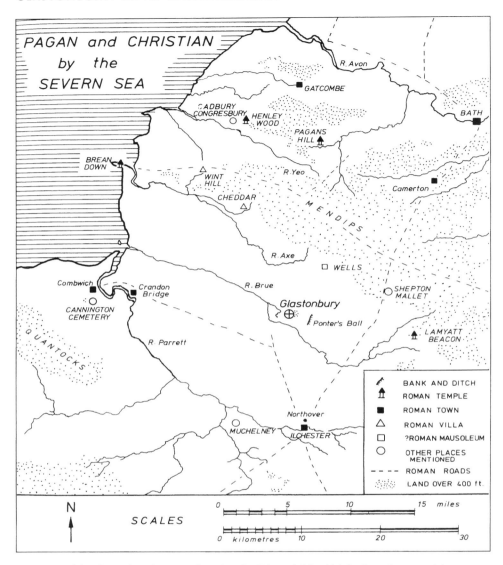

17 *Maps of the places where there is evidence (mostly slight and debatable) for the early stages of the Christian conversion of Somerset*

There are, additionally, possible Christian features in the large cemetery at Cannington, west of the River Parrett (see **17**); this was used from the fourth to the eighth centuries AD. The cemetery at Northover, near Ilchester, may also prove to be Christian, but it has not yet been fully excavated.

Although there may have been Christians and partly Christian cemeteries in Somerset in the Roman period, there is no evidence that any organised religion survived into later centuries from this source. We should look for the origins of Christian Glastonbury to three quite difference influences: to the evangelising activities of western missionaries (from early 'British' Christianity established in Wales and Ireland in the fifth and sixth centuries – the 'St Patrick' syndrome); to influences disseminated from the Christian civilisations of the Mediterranean, directly, by sea (for which relevant archaeological evidence will be cited below, p.71); and, later, to the English Church established by Augustine in Kent in the later sixth and seventh centuries AD.

The possibility of an early Christian use of the Tor as a hermitage in pre-Saxon times – in the sixth century – is discussed in chapter 6. Two other small buildings in Somerset, at Brean Down and Lamyatt Beacon, are also claimed to be Christian chapels of the early post-Roman period; both were adjacent to late Roman temples and both had graves close by. There is also the possibility of post-Roman Christian use of the temple at Pagans Hill.

Another place that may be of Christian origin, associated with 'British' rather than 'English' evangelizing activity, is close to Glastonbury, at Street, on the south side of the causeway linking these two settlements. Here (at what is now Leigh) is the site of *Lantokay* (or *Lantocai*), the name known from documentary sources as early as the late seventh century; this is associated with St Cai. The prefix LAN is the equivalent of Welsh LLAN, denoting an early Christian enclosure or chapel/church nucleus; *Lantokay* is the only LAN name in the area. The site is presumed to be that of the present church; its large churchyard may originally have been ovoid or circular, another feature of early Christian sites in the west of Britain. It may also be relevant that just to the west is said to be the site of the old manor house – *Brutessayshe* (British Ash) in the perambulations of the Abbey's estates (p.146) and the starting point for the 'walk'. Also, a short distance west again is Walton; the prefix WAL appears to denote a British ('Welsh') settlement surviving in a predominantly Anglo-Saxon area of settlements.

It is, however, with the expansion of the English church that Glastonbury enters documentary history, when the king of Anglo-Saxon Wessex, Ina, gave his royal support to what was perhaps already a Christian centre. It is these origins of Christian Glastonbury, in the sixth and later centuries, that figure prominently in later chapters.

4

GLASTONBURY IN WRITTEN SOURCES

Now lest I weary my readers with conjectures of little value, we will proceed with the solid truth

William of Malmesbury, earlier twelfth century

Introduction

This is no place, nor is there space, to include yet another potted history of Glastonbury. The written sources are moreover too complex to be summarised briefly. It was, however, the twelfth century that was particularly important for forging the character of many monastic 'histories'; and the writings of that time still shape the modern historiography of Glastonbury. The world view of the medieval writers coloured their perception of history, fable, legend and myth: fact or fiction. Many claims that appear to make Glastonbury extraordinary are seen to be commonplace when placed in a wider historical perspective. All that can be done in this chapter is to indicate the character of the written sources, and thus something of the broader framework within which Glastonbury must be viewed. Also stressed are details of the history that are relevant to the physical aspects and material culture of the site. Some historical material will be found in later chapters linked to specific sites, buildings or topics; and especially to what has been revealed by archaeology.

The Roman and pagan/early Christian background has been discussed in the previous chapter. The Dark Age history and archaeology of Somerset as a whole are briefly mentioned in connection with the Tor in chapter 6. The sparse written sources for this period, the fifth and sixth centuries, are very difficult to interpret; modern historians warn archaeologists not to use them uncritically, as several have.

Written sources for the pre-Conquest period for Glastonbury are principally related to the Abbey. They include charters, *Lives* of saints, letters, inscriptions and the *Anglo-Saxon Chronicle*. Many other documents from which a detailed history of the Abbey could have been written have been lost. Numerous books were destroyed in the fire of 1184; and many more were lost at the time of the

Dissolution. Part of a Glastonbury manuscript was discovered by an Oxford antiquarian in 1722 when some tobacco was sent to him, wrapped in a page from it!

The charters were principally concerned with land grants. From them has been built, by numerous scholars, a massive edifice concerning the estates of the Abbey (see chapter 9) and its abbots and benefactors. There are, of course, problems in deciding which are genuine documents of the time to which they purport to relate, and which are later copies, with additions and alterations. The purpose of such forgeries was to legitimise claims to land which might otherwise be dubious. The earliest charters for the Abbey estates which are generally agreed to be genuine are of the late seventh century. This is the oldest date for the Abbey's existence which can be relied upon; and as will be seen in chapter 7, there is little or no archaeological evidence for anything earlier in the Abbey, although there is on the Tor (chapter 6).

The *Anglo-Saxon Chronicle* was a compilation of events and although much of it provides valuable historical clues, it was not written down before the late Anglo-Saxon period; it does, however, confirm an eighth-century or earlier date for the Abbey, in connection with the church built by King Ina (chapter 7), a royal patronage that was not unique to Glastonbury.

Two special sources, which are considered at more length below, are epigraphic. The first is that of inscriptions on two 'pyramids' (p.41). These were possibly as early as the eighth or ninth centuries, but were not 'read' until the twelfth, by which time they were heavily eroded. The second is a brass plate (p.43), on which was inscribed a brief history of the Abbey, for the benefit of pilgrims and other visitors in the late fourteenth or fifteenth century. One of the key texts for the tenth century is the *Life of St Dunstan*; by the twelfth century there were five versions of this. He is the major historical figure associated with Glastonbury before the Normans. While the *Life* does not rank as reliable history, it does provide a date before which certain matters were being discussed, even if they were not all actually true.

After the Conquest, there is a wealth of documentation for both Abbey and town. The crucial sources are the chronicles or histories written from the twelfth century onwards, each one an embellishment and amplification of the last. They are not the same as a modern historian would write; they are instead more about the past as it was felt it should have been (see chapter 5).

The earliest of these, the *De Antiquitate . . . or Concerning the Early History of the Church of Glastonbury*, is the one most relied on by historians (both medieval and modern); it was written by William of Malmesbury, a writer famous in his own day and the most comprehensive English historian since Bede. He visited the Abbey and compiled its history from the materials he was presented with by the monks, who commissioned the work in the early twelfth century; he also made out what he could of the inscriptions on the pyramids. He was a careful worker, and where sceptical, he allowed this to be read into his words; but even his work must be seen in the context of contemporary attitudes towards the truth.

The original text of his history of the Abbey (which does not survive) was manipulated and added to in later centuries, so that it is difficult to be sure what is original. Some help is given, however, where the same material is used in his other works. Commentaries on William, like the charters, form a massive element in modern historical writing on Glastonbury.

The later abbey chroniclers, Adam of Domerham and John of Glastonbury, incorporated much of William's text, and added material likely to enhance the reputation of the Abbey, as will be seen in chapter 5. They are of course an invaluable source for the events of their own day, and as a record of what 'history' was being promoted throughout the Middle Ages. For the closing years of the Abbey, we have the information collected by Henry VIII's commissioners, in some respects a very detailed account.

There are also, from the fifteenth century onwards, travellers' accounts. The fame of Glastonbury was such that most major English travellers visited the Abbey and town. From more recent centuries, major histories occur in the writings of William Camden and others; and eventually there are maps.

It must be stressed that the historiography of the written sources for Glastonbury is massive (see Further Reading, p.169). What has been distilled from it for present purposes is not authoritative. Nor, in a book of this kind, can it be referenced; but it will hopefully lead the reader to the more serious works on the history of Glastonbury. A basic point will first be considered – what is the origin of the name of Glastonbury?

The names of Glastonbury (Anglo-Saxon *Glestingaburg*)

The suffix '-bury' is very common in place-names. It derives from Anglo-Saxon *byrig*, which can mean either a strong place (for instance the hillforts such as South Cadbury) or a monastery (such as Congresbury = 'St Congar's bury'). Either meaning could apply to Glastonbury. The origin of the *Glaston*- prefix is not known; the name is first used in charters in the late seventh–early eighth century. Later traditions provided explanations for the name. The best-known concerns one *Glasteing*, a man said to have come from the north of Britain. He pursued a sow to Glastonbury and finally found her suckling her piglets next to the Old Church, under a fruit tree. The sow story is one which occurs in many saints' lives, but the possibility remains that someone called *Glast* or similar was the lord of the estate, which was named after him, as so many Anglo-Saxon places and estates were; and that he settled here with his own people, the *inga* element; hence the monastery or strong place of the *Glestingas* – possibly both (see chapter 6).

The name *Inyswitrin* (often suggested to be British or Gaelic) is equated with Glastonbury in a charter supposed to be dated to 601; this is, however, regarded by modern historians as spurious and the name is not really mentioned until Gerald of Wales uses it in the late twelfth century. The *inys* part means 'island'; in the fifteenth century *witrin* was equated with Latin *vitreus* = glass (hence vitreous) and it was but a short step to link this to the *glas* of Glastonbury = *the Island of Glass*.

Visitors to Glastonbury today are greeted with a roadside notice telling them they have arrived at the ancient *Island of Avalon*. This name was, in Arthurian legend, the place where Arthur went to die. The name is known in both French and Welsh medieval sources, either a personal name (for instance *Avalloc*) or as meaning 'the island of apples'. The name as first linked with Arthur by Geoffrey of Monmouth and to Arthur *and* Glastonbury by Gerald of Wales, in the twelfth century. It was fused with the *Glasteing* story by 'apples of the most precious sort' which Arthur was supposed to have found there. The name *Avalon* is also on the lead cross from Arthur's grave (below, p.58). Its identification with the Glastonbury area was very much part of the promotion of the claim that Arthur was buried in the Abbey (see the next chapter).

Anglo-Saxon Glastonbury

The principal places related to the English settlement of Somerset are shown in **18**. They include the 'battles', episodes of confrontation; the palaces, where the king met his counsellors; and the monasteries known to have been founded before the Norman Conquest. Of the latter, Glastonbury became the most important. The patronage of one of the earliest kings of Wessex, Ina, has been noted; and it continued to be linked with the consolidation of the English church and state, as was the neighbouring bishopric of Bath (later with Wells).

The earlier abbots of Glastonbury included some with British personal names, as well as some with English ones; and while too much cannot be made of this in 'racial' terms, it remains possible that the Abbey had British origins in the later seventh century, before the advent of Anglo-Saxon domination. The significance of the British monastery or stronghold on the Tor in the sixth century is fundamental in this discussion, although there need not be continuity between the two places (see chapter 6).

The succession of early abbots has been reconstructed at least partially from charter and other evidence; it is also possibly reflected in some of the names on the pyramids (p.42). These, and the excavated churches of the eighth to tenth centuries, are (or were) the principal physical expression of the early history of the Abbey.

In the ninth century, the security of the area was seriously threatened by the struggle between Wessex and the Danish armies under King Guthrum. Glastonbury must have been very vulnerable when King Alfred was forced to retreat into his marshland stronghold at Athelney (south of Glastonbury, see **18**). Alfred's victory in 871 and the conversion of the Danish king brought renewed peace. The events of the reconciliation are linked to Wedmore and possibly to nearby Cheddar, where a hall and other buildings of this period have been excavated.

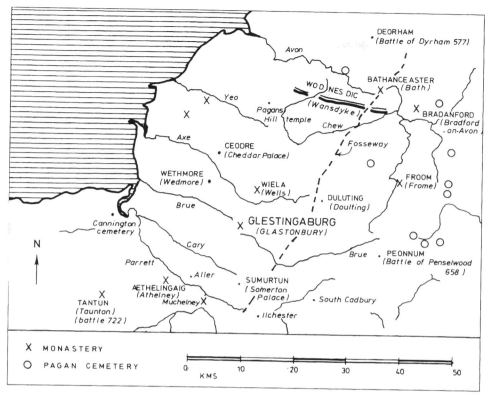

18 *Places in Somerset with evidence of Anglo-Saxon use, or named in Anglo-Saxon written sources. Some have been excavated, such as Cheddar, Wells and Glastonbury.* After PAR, 1992

It has been suggested by historians that the Abbey was in a run–down state in this period, in the ninth and earlier tenth centuries; but a great era was then initiated by Abbot Dunstan. Before proceeding to his contribution, we should firstly make a brief diversion to look at inscriptions on the pyramids and the brass plate; the former probably pre-dates Dunstan and the latter may conveniently be dealt with at the same time.

The 'pyramids'

The word 'pyramid' is used in the Glastonbury written sources, and by all later writers down to the present day, to mean structures either over, or marking the location of, early graves or tomb-shrines (see **48**). The word is also used by some writers for the tomb-shrines themselves, that is stone structures above or around the graves themselves, at, or just above, ground-level.

The connection between this use of the word and its more familiar use to define a geometrical figure, or the great stone pyramids of Egypt, has been well expressed in relation to both of the above meanings: 'any structure tapering upwards from a broad base to a narrower summit, like a coped tomb, or like the sculptured crosses of Northern Britain and Ireland'. Used in this sense for *interior* memorials, at Glastonbury a 'pyramid' was said to enclose the body of St Patrick, 'on the right side of the altar' (later 'clothed with silver') and also St Indracht on the left. No evidence of these internal memorials survived later rebuildings. Here we are more concerned with the *external* memorial pyramids and the confusion concerning them.

William of Malmesbury (p.38) was the first writer to describe the 'pyramids' of Glastonbury; these were still extant, albeit very weathered, when he wrote in the earlier twelfth century. One had five stages, the other four. These were, according to William, decorated with certain sculptures in relief, and with a series of names (**19**). There are variant versions of some names in different manuscripts of William; the translations given below (that from the taller pyramid followed by the shorter) are from *John of Glastonbury*:

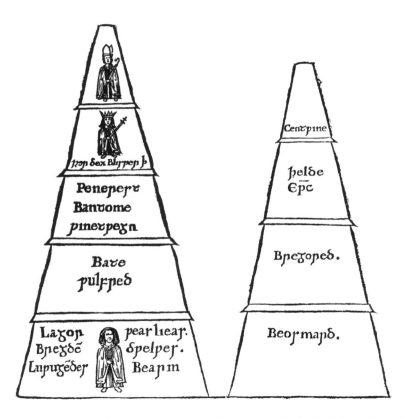

19 *Henry Spelman's seventeenth-century reconstruction of the two pyramids; he based this on the earlier written description of William of Malmesbury*

. . . in the topmost storey is an image fashioned in episcopal guise. In the second an image exhibiting royal pomp, and the letters HER . . ., SEXI . . ., BLIS. In the third indeed the names: WEMCREST, BANTOMP, WINETHEGN. In the fourth: HATE, WULFRED, EANFLED. In the fifth which is the lowest, an image and these words: LOGWOR, WESLICAS, BREGDEN, SWELWES, HWINGENDES, BERN, ALTERA . . . four storeys, on which are written these words: HEDDE EPISCOPUS, BREGORED, BEORUUARD.

Attempts have been made by various scholars to identify the persons named. On the smaller pyramid, *Haeddi* was a famous bishop of Winchester; Bregored may have been an early bishop with a British name; and Beorhtwald was the first abbot with an Anglo-Saxon name. The names on the taller one have also been partly identified with the early secular or ecclesiastical dignitaries and there have been many attempts to link these names with people known from other sources. Aelrid Watkin suggested that the pyramids commemorated (probably at a later date) a visit to Glastonbury in the 670s by St Wilfred and Queen Eanflede, in the context of the former's attempt to impose the usage of the Roman church in the West. There is no actual record of such a visit, but this could account for two of the inscribed names.

It may finally be asked what was the date of the pyramids – clearly they belong to some time before William's day. A date between the late seventh and twelfth centuries is indicated. If, as may be guessed from the dates of other high crosses, they might be of the eighth or ninth centuries, they were retained in the time of Dunstan. They may have been partly buried (or were reset) in the layer of clay (laid down at Dunstan's direction) to raise the level of the cemetery (p.71). The location of the pyramids, and their appearance, is further considered in chapter 7.

The brass plate

This plate was set up on a pillar. Its physical characteristics, its location and archaeological context are discussed in chapter 7 (p.91). Here we are concerned with the inscription on it (**20**). This is in medieval Latin characters of the late fourteenth or fifteenth century. It recapitulates the legendary history of the Abbey from the time of Joseph of Arimathea. St David's supposed addition to the Old Church is mentioned, and the text concludes:

And lest the site or size of the earlier church should come to be forgotten because of such additions, he [St David] erected this column on a line drawn southwards through the two eastern angles of the same church, and cutting it off from the aforesaid chancel. And its length was

20 *Brass plate, recording detail of the history of the Abbey (inscribed in the fourteenth or fifteenth century); the shape is rather like a head and shoulders image, or a cross on a stepped base*

60ft westward from that line, its breadth was truly 26ft; the distance from the centre of this pillar from the midpoint between the aforesaid angles, 48ft.

The interest of the inscription is firstly that it is a guide to what history was being promoted in the late fourteenth to fifteenth century; and secondly that it perpetuated an older tradition of the dimensions and location of the Old Church (the *vetusta ecclesia*); this is discussed further in relation to that building below, on p.90).

Dunstan

Dunstan was of noble birth; he numbered two English bishops among his kin and was a relative of King Athelstan; he was probably born *c*.910 at Baltonsborough, a little to the east of Glastonbury and an estate of the Abbey. In the 930s he was at the court of Athelstan; this was held periodically at Cheddar, Frome and other local places. After the latter's death in 939, Dunstan became a chaplain or counsellor to the young King Edmund. He had by this time become imbued with the spirit of reform, a movement initiated on the Continent and immensely influential in England in the tenth century. His strict views, however, made him very unpopular with Edmund and the young nobles at court; but a famous story relates how, c.940, when he was at Cheddar, the king went hunting on Mendip, and his horse, following a stag, was about to plunge into Cheddar Gorge. The king, in mortal danger, repented of having been unjust to Dunstan, the horse pulled up short of the abyss and Edmund appointed Dunstan to the abbacy of Glastonbury: this proved to be a major landmark in the monastic history of England.

The Abbey, which had been in decline, was now restored, and brought strictly under a new version of the Rule of St Benedict; this was adhered to for the rest of the Abbey's life. Dunstan subsequently became Archbishop of Canterbury and continued to be a leading figure of the Reform movement. At King Edgar's coronation feast in 959, Dunstan's puritanism had achieved such power that 'he alone dared to drag the dissolute king back to the table from the embraces of a mother and daughter'! The physical expression of Dunstan's work at Glastonbury was the enlargement of the church, and the creation of an early form of claustral layout. These have been located by excavation (chapter 7). He also raised the level of the ancient cemetery, so that 'the saints could rest in peace'. He was, however, far more than a spiritual leader; he was also very interested in the technology of craft and industry, and in music. William of Malmesbury refers to organs and bells he made, while John of Glastonbury records that in a little shed with a lean-to roof:

> . . . he applied his hands to his work, his lips to the psalms, and his mind to heaven. The stylus ran over the surface of the tablet, the pen over the page. He took up the brush to paint and the chisel to carve. Indeed, in Glastonbury there are, according to tradition, altar cloths, crosses, thuribles, phials, chasubles and other vestments of his workmanship . . .

John also tells of Dunstan's reaction to being tempted by the devil, when he 'quickly plunged a pair of iron tongs into a furnace'. These skills may also be reflected in some of the features and artefacts found in excavation (p.115).

His influence was long felt at Glastonbury, although he was primarily associated with Canterbury. In the fourteenth century, a book was referred to in a Glastonbury source as St Dunstan's because of its decorative binding. This, including an ivory crucifix, was regarded as his own work. 'Dunstan's Ditch' is a feature that recurs as a landmark in medieval documents of the town (see **63**).

Glastonbury after the Norman Conquest

The early years after the Conquest were difficult ones for the Abbey. In the great survey of England's taxable wealth, the Domesday Book, Glastonbury is nevertheless the wealthiest monastic house, although its fortunes did not fully revive until the time of Henri de Blois (see below).

The first Norman abbot (1082) was Turstin, who had been a monk at Caen. He sowed discord by removing ancient customs and replacing them with others of his own country. Among other irritations, he made the monks abandon the Gregorian chant and forced them to sing that of William of Fécamp. Encountering opposition to this and other changes, he resorted to force. William of Malmesbury's account (written a decade or two later) is worth quoting verbatim; it is relevant to our understanding of what the church may have been like in the eleventh century:

> One day he came into the chapter in a turmoil and fiercely berated the monks about these and other matters without being able to bend them to his will. Forthwith he became beside himself with rage and had his soldiers and armed attendants summoned. At this sight the monks were seized with extreme fear and took flight as best they could, making their way to the church for sanctuary and blockading its doors with bars. But the servants of Belial burst into the temple and perpetrated unheard-of wickedness. They pursued the monks even up to the altar, where they had fled to beseech divine assistance with flowing tears, and assailed them with bows and arrows. Some of them even climbed on to the triforium galleries between the columns so that they might more easily sate their wicked souls with blood. Neither reverence for that place nor for its saints could hinder them until they had transfixed one monk with a lance as he was embracing the holy altar, killed another at the base of the altar by piercing him with arrows, and seriously wounded fourteen others.

Turstin began a new church (see **55**), but did not live to complete it. His work was abandoned by Herlewin (1101) who began to build a much larger church (completed *c*.1140).

The next important abbot was Henri de Blois, an aristocrat and scholar, who ruled the Abbey for a very long period (1126-71). The buildings were in a state of collapse (reminding him of the dwellings of peasants), and he set about restoring them, together with the finances of the Abbey. He was responsible for many new buildings, including a bell tower, chapter house, cloister, lavatory, refectory, dormitory, the infirmary with its chapel, a castellum (a princely 'castle'-like structure within the grounds), an outer gate, a brewery and stabling for horses. As well as concerning himself with monastic discipline, he also presented many rich gifts to the Abbey; and he took a keen interest in its estates. He said of one, in the Levels:

> in it I saw red corn, the colour of gold, rustling pleasantly in the gentle breeze, its surface sweeping the level as there were no weeds in it.

He was a patron of William of Malmesbury and Gerald of Wales, and gave over forty books to the library. He had, however, a love of luxury ill-suited to the basic ethics of monastic life, which earned him the epithets of 'a rival pope, the old wizard of Winchester'. After his death, on St Urban's Day (25 May) 1184, there was a devastating fire at Glastonbury which destroyed most of the buildings, including the Old Church, and many of the relics, vestments, books and other wealth of the Abbey.

Rebuilding began immediately. The site of the Old Church was commemorated by the magnificent new Lady Chapel, generally believed in medieval times not only to have been built on the precise spot where the earlier building had stood, but to be of similar dimensions. The correlation was recorded on the brass plate set up in the late fourteenth or fifteenth century, described above (see p.43). The Lady Chapel was consecrated on 11 June 1186; but it is doubtful whether it could have been completed by this time.

The fire initiated a period of crisis for the Abbey; large sums were required for the rebuilding. Henry II authorised his chamberlain Ralph Fitzstephen to spend all the Abbey revenues on the rebuild. Ralph translated the remains of St Patrick and St Indracht from the Old Church into new shrines; and the bones of Dunstan were also 'discovered' at this time (below, p.56). Henry II died in 1189, and Ralph soon afterwards. The need to raise the status of the Abbey, to protect its possessions and to attract pilgrims, led to the exhumation of 'Arthur' in 1191 (p.55 below).

Financial problems were not the only ones. Henri de Soilly, the abbot who had ordered the exhumation, became Bishop of Worcester in 1193. His successor Savaric had been appointed Bishop of Bath; he attempted, by also becoming Abbot of Glastonbury, to make it little more than a 'bishop's monastery'. He achieved this by armed force, involving beatings and tortures of the monks who opposed him. It was only by the intervention of Pope Honorius III that the union of Bath and Glastonbury was quashed. Savaric nevertheless had improved monastic discipline and lessened excessive luxury; when the union between the bishopric and abbey was dissolved, one of the measures reintroduced was stronger beer at Glastonbury!

The subsequent fortunes of the Abbey in the thirteenth to fifteenth centuries need not be elaborated. This period saw the completion of the great church which was extended eastwards from the Lady Chapel; the consolidation and expansion of the Abbey estates; and the construction of many new works such as seawalls and mills. This was the golden age of the Abbey. From this period, apart from the ruins of the church itself, the tower of St Michael survives on the Tor and excavations have recovered the plan of its nave (chapter 6) and also that of the chapel at Beckery (chapter 9). A few buildings of this time survive in the town, and much of the precinct walls (chapters 7 and 8).

One of the greatest abbots at the end of this period was Richard Bere, installed in 1494, regarded by some historians as the foremost abbot since Dunstan. He was responsible for major new buildings in the Abbey. With the addition of the Edgar Chapel at the east end, Glastonbury became the longest ecclesiastical building in

England. Some buildings outside the precinct and in the town are attributed to him, including the present church of St Benignus (p.130). He was also a very learned man; copies were made at his behest of the *Chronicle* of John of Glastonbury; and the cult of Joseph of Arimathea was vigorously promoted.

Of especial relevance to the archaeology of the Abbey was his work on the crypt under the Lady Chapel, referred to in 1520 as St Joseph's Chapel (a name now popularly applied to the whole building). This also destroyed the site of the Old Church, which might otherwise have yielded crucial evidence to archaeologists.

The Dissolution and its aftermath

The final abbot was Richard Whiting (1525-39). In the last part of his abbacy, external pressures associated with the Dissolution had weakened morale. A bishop's visitation in 1538 heard complaints which indicate the tensions that had accumulated among the community. By the summer of 1539, the Abbey was the last to survive in Somerset, but it was doomed.

Whiting was by that time in his mid-seventies, 'but a weak man and sickly'. Interrogation at Sharpham (a manor near Glastonbury) was followed by removal to the Tower of London. Accusations against him were relatively trivial, but included the popular idea that he had hidden treasure. At his trial on 14 November 1539, at Wells, a charge of robbery replaced that of treason. A contemporary account relates that:

> on November 15, together with John Thorne, the treasurer, and the young monk named Roger Wilfrid, he was taken across the moors to Glastonbury. At the abbey gates he was attached to a hurdle and dragged through the town and up the Tor, where three gallows had been set up . . . the abbot remained silent.

Carley concludes:

> At the best of times the Tor presents a daunting spectacle; in the late autumn with a constant wind blowing it has a formidable, almost supernatural aspect . . . Whiting's age and gentleness must have made a stark contrast to the barrenness of the hill and the brutality of his tormentors. Indeed in some ways the hanging can almost symbolise the ending of the English monastic movement; and the Tor witnessed on this wild November day the apotheosis of the Crucifixion scene in the medieval mystery plays . . . As soon as he was dead, Whiting's head was struck off and his body cut into quarters; one to be displayed at Wells, one at Bath, one at Ilchester and one at Bridgwater. The head was placed over the great gateway of the Abbey itself.

The account of the execution by Dom David Knowles is also evocative of several themes in this book (though rather uncharacteristic of this great monastic historian):

> When Whiting rode up to London his orchards had been red with fruit; now, the last splendours had been swept even from the sheltered woods of Dinder, and the trees near the abbey were bare. The old man's eyes, as he stood beneath the gallows, would have travelled for the last time along the slopes of the clouded hills to Brent Knoll and Steep Holm; over the grey expanse of mere to the sharp outline of the Quantocks and the darker Poldens; over the distant ridges to the south where the Glastonbury manors near Domerham had been white with sheep, and over those to the north once hallowed, so the story ran, by the footsteps of the 'beauteous Lamb of God'. No other landscape in all England carried so great a weight of legend. To the island valley at his feet the dying Arthur had been ferried. Through sedges from the Parrett had come Joseph of Arimathea bearing the Grail. On the pleasant pastures of Mendip had shone the countenance of the Child Jesus. Below him lay the now majestic pile of his abbey, desolate, solitary, and about to crumble into ruins.

The Abbey's property had been valued in 1535 at the considerable sum of £3301 7s 4d, still the wealthiest in the land. Many objects do seem to have been hidden – treasure-seekers made a rich haul from walls, vaults and other secret places and a total of 488 objects was recovered in 1539, including a gold chalice; these were said to have been hidden from previous Commissioners. Apart from the portable items, real estate included a 'house' that was 'princely, mete for the King's majesty', with four parks and a 'great . . . mere with pike, bream, perch and roach'; and four fine manor houses, together with woods, fisheries and swanneries (for the estates see chapter 9).

The Commissioners wrote to Thomas Cromwell (Henry VIII's agent) that they had dispatched the servants with half a year's wages; and 'with the king's benevolence and reward' assigned pensions to the monks. 'We find them very glad to depart, most humbly thanking the king's majesty'.

After Henry VIII's death in 1547, Edward VI granted the ruins to Edward Seymour, Duke of Somerset. Much had already been removed, including roof lead, glass and dressed stone. Edward settled a colony of Protestant Dutch weavers (Walloons) in the grounds in 1550; they built two dye houses, a brew house and a bakehouse. The Abbot's kitchen alone survived intact, being used later as a Quaker meeting house.

The area of the precinct passed through various lay hands in later centuries until the sale of 1907 (p.85). Depredations continued, and damage to both buildings and archaeological deposits was severe. One episode is reflected by finds in the excavations: dead dogs and other rubbish buried after Monmouth and his army camped in the grounds in 1685. Less and less remained for visitors to see; but many important travellers came to Glastonbury to see what survived of its former fame. Another major episode of destruction was in 1792-94, when many loads of stone were taken for the new road to Wells; the workmen sold capitals, corbels and sculpture to passing visitors.

Visitors to Glastonbury

The fame of Glastonbury attracted many English travellers; their observations are an important addition to the earlier written sources. Not only did they observe and record what they saw, but also what they were told. From them we can reconstruct the history of the popular tales as they were passed down the generations.

The first to record after William of Malmesbury was William of Worcester in 1480; he asked the monks for details of all the chronicles, in particular for anything concerning King Arthur. He was an inveterate measurer of streets and buildings; his dimensions for the late fifteenth century are invaluable – where it is possible to check them; here and elsewhere, they have proved to be remarkably reliable. He gives a precise location for the pyramids (p.114), describing them as 'two stone crosses hollowed out where they laid King Arthur's bones, and where . . . lies Joseph of Arimathea'.

Another traveller who saw the Abbey and Arthur's tomb before the Dissolution was John Leland. He had visited in 1533, and was entertained by Whiting; he admired what he saw, especially the wealth and antiquity of its books. On a second visit in 1542 he does not even mention the Abbey, which was now being dismantled; only the town, with its market and churches, is described.

Celia Fiennes travelled southern England in the late seventeenth century. She:

> ascended a stony hill and went just by the tower: . . . like a Beacon; it had Bells formerly on it, and some supersticion observ'd there . . . from this I descended a very steep stony way into the town . . . where was founded the first monastery . . . now a ragged poor place . . . there is the Holy Thorn growing on a chimney.

She climbed the tower of St John, and again remarks on 'the prospect of the place which appeared very ragged and decayed.'

William Stukeley came in 1723. He deplored what he saw:

> A presbyterian tenant has made more barbarous havock there, than has been since the Dissolution; for every week a pillar, a buttress, a window . . . jamb, or an angle of fine hewn stone is sold to the best bidder; whilst I was there they were excoriating St Joseph's Chapel for that purpose,

and the squared stones were laid up by lots in the abbot's kitchen; the rest goes to paving yards and stalls for cattle or the highway.

On the north side is St Mary's Chapel . . . the roof beat down by violence, and a sorry wooden one in its place, thatched with stubble to make it serve as a stable; the manger lies upon the altar and niche where they put the holy water.

The crypt of the Lady Chapel he found full of water (see p.28): 'here was a capacious receptacle for the dead; they have taken up many lead coffins, and melted them into cisterns'.

Stukeley's great contribution was his drawings, which are our best source for the appearance of the peninsula, Ponter's Ball (p.26), the Abbey and the Tor (see **40**). After this, histories and accounts of the place proliferate; but not until the nineteenth century are the beginnings of scholarly study to be seen (see chapter 7).

Conclusion

There has been a succession of learned (and other) studies on the written sources, extending down to the present day; clearly the ramifications are far from being exhausted, even if the discovery of new documents is nowadays rare. It is, however, by no means the case with archaeology, where what has been discovered to date is a small fraction of what still lies buried beneath the ground. Historians have been reluctant to get to grips with the difficult task of understanding archaeology – to them an alien discipline. In the case of the Abbey there is the additional problem that the work there has never been properly published. The task therefore of integrating the results of two very different kinds of data has hardly been attempted: this book is no more than an introduction to the problems, which will keep both historians and archaeologists occupied well into the future.

5

MYTH AND LEGEND

There is a continuum from theories that probably are not true, but easily could be, to theories that could only be true at the cost of overthrowing large edifices of successful orthodox science

R. Dawkins, 1986

The Cross . . . marks a Christian sanctuary, so ancient that only legend can record its origin

Noticeboard in the Abbey grounds

Believers and sceptics: the attraction of the irrational

There is inevitably overlap between this chapter and the last. The development of myth, and the political, economic and religious contexts of its development, are matters of great interest to the historian. So too are attempts to discern any basis of real fact which may lie behind picturesque but implausible stories. Confusion arises when the myths are elevated to facts, and believed in more or less literally. Most, if not all, of the myths associated with Glastonbury are a compendium of invention of medieval and later centuries. The visits to Glastonbury (or burial there) of such people as Joseph of Arimathea, or King Arthur, are not mentioned in historical sources until many hundreds of years after they were supposed to have taken place. In the following pages, we shall consider when, how and why the better-known stories appeared, and the varying degrees of probability they attract. Some associations, such as that of St Indracht, are more historically plausible than for instance, that of St Joseph; and cases have been made out for medieval traditions (such as that for a pre-Anglo-Saxon church) being based on older finds, now-vanished documents, or oral traditions.

However improbable, the Glastonbury myths have taken root, partly through being repeated so many times, by the medieval chroniclers in medieval and later literature, and by subsequent writers. They are very persistent down to the present day, being regarded as true by the great majority of visitors and writers; or if not 'true', then very attractive.

Attitudes to Glastonbury myths may be categorised as follows, in order of credibility:

1 They are true in an absolute sense, and are based on factual occurrences, even if there is no citable historical or archaeological fact; this in some cases amounts to a statement of faith ('I believe in King Arthur' T-shirt).

2 While not absolutely true in every detail, they are based on some real historical events which have become exaggerated or garbled with the passage of time; this is the 'no-smoke-without-fire' school of thought.

3 Even if not true, they ought to be; and the affirmation of their historicity is important to enrich our cultural heritage; and in particular that of Glastonbury. This is well expressed by a recent scholar: 'The Glastonbury stories contain grains of profound truth even if they are historically inaccurate: they are exemplary tales, which portray a past as it should have been.'

4 They are not actually true, but wouldn't it be nice if they were! ('and did those Feet?'); the same scholar quoted above writes: 'those who can trace Joseph of Arimathea's footsteps on Wirrall Hill or detect the Holy Blood in the reddish tinge of the water flowing from Chalice Well are the fortunate ones; they are the emperors of the Glastonbury Kingdom.'

5 They are true in a symbolic way in expressing real spiritual values; and they have, moreover, given rise to some remarkable medieval art, poetry and other literature.

6 They are not actually true, but they are a good way of attracting money and people to Glastonbury (very common).

7 They are not true, but are wholly the product of medieval and later invention, for pecuniary, political or prestige motives; their continued exposition as fact degrades real scholarship and historical truth, which should be exciting enough without the embroidery of myth elevated to fact.

It need hardly be said that the last viewpoint is that of the authors; this book attempts to show what the historical and archaeological facts about Glastonbury really are. The myths are, however, interesting to the scholar, for what they tell us about medieval and later aspirations and thoughts. A historian must record when people believed what, and if possible why; but not confuse the myth with what actually happened. Glastonbury is not unique here, but must be seen in a wider perspective of such activities in religious contexts throughout the world, and especially in medieval Europe.

Arthur's grave and shrine

The name of Arthur occurs in written sources before the Norman Conquest; but he gained prominence in romanticised 'Norman-Celtic' writing, especially in Geoffrey of Monmouth's extremely popular *History of the Kings of Britain* compiled in the earlier twelfth century. He was first associated with Glastonbury by Caradoc of Llancarfan in the earlier twelfth century; and it is not until the later twelfth that his grave was located there. Most significantly there is no mention of him in relation to Glastonbury in the original editions of William of Malmesbury, who was at some pains to include everything the monks told him about the early history of the Abbey; nor is any association suggested by Geoffrey of Monmouth, writing also at this time.

In 1191, however, Abbot Henry de Soilly ordered his monks to dig between the two pyramids (p.114). He may have done so on the advice of King Henry II, although the king died before the exhumation began. Henry had apparently acquired secret information from 'an ancient Welsh bard' concerning the position of where to dig and how deeply.

The exhumation took place seven years after the destruction of the Abbey by the great fire of 1184. The earliest account of the excavation is by Gerald of Wales, writing originally before 1192. He seems to have been an eye-witness of the work; his text may be quoted verbatim (**colour plate 13**).

> Now the body of King Arthur . . . was found in our own days at Glastonbury, deep down in the earth and encoffined in a hollow oak between two stone pyramids . . . in the grave was a cross of lead, placed under a stone and not above it, but fixed on the under side . . . I have felt the letters engraved thereon, which do not project or stand out, but are turned inwards towards the stone. They run as follows:
>
> 'Here lies buried the renowned King Arthur, with Guinevere his second wife, in the isle of Avalon' . . . two parts of the tomb, to wit, the head, were allotted to the bones of the man, while the remaining third towards the foot contained the bones of the woman in a place apart; and there was found a yellow tress of woman's hair still retaining its colour and freshness; but when a certain monk snatched it and lifted it with greedy hand, it straightway all of it fell into dust . . . the bones of Arthur . . . were so huge . . . his shank-bone when placed against that of the tallest man in the place . . . reached a good three inches above his knee . . . the eye-socket was a good palm in width . . . there were ten wounds or more, all of which were scarred over, save one larger than the rest, which had made a great hole.

Professor Leslie Alcock and Dr Ralegh Radford have argued that the exhumation really did find Arthur, if not Guinevere (below, p.58). They believe not only that Arthur was a historical figure, but also that he was buried at Glastonbury. Most scholarly opinion, however, believes that the whole thing was a hoax. Antonia Gransden has coolly demolished the arguments for authenticity; her reasons are incorporated in what follows.

Why, it may be asked, should such an elaborate spectacle have been staged? One answer is that all abbeys were, in general, anxious to preserve and expand their prestige by claiming association with saints and other notable figures of the past, and by their possession of relics – and Arthur had not already been claimed by anyone else. But there were also reasons more pressing for the monks at Glastonbury.

The years 1184-92 were a crisis period for the Abbey. Drastic measures were required to increase resources after the fire, to attract pilgrims from far and wide. The monks would have hoped to emulate the remarkable success of Canterbury in establishing the cult of St Thomas a Becket, murdered in 1170; the monks there also badly needed money to rebuild after the Canterbury fire of 1174; attractions included phials said to hold diluted blood of St Thomas, which were on sale to pilgrims.

Canterbury also provided an exemplar in its exhumation of Dunstan in 1070, buried at a considerable depth. This too had yielded an inscribed lead tablet clearly identifying the remains; and the grave had a 'pyramid' set over it.

Glastonbury also claimed to possess the relics of Dunstan, said to have been stolen from Canterbury in the earlier twelfth century, and 'hidden'. This was an unlikely story, and scornfully denied by Canterbury; the bones claimed as those of Dunstan were nevertheless also conveniently exhumed after the fire at Glastonbury, to further prestige and attract money.

The establishment of an Arthurian cult would, it was hoped, secure such aims. The English kings would also have found this useful in their efforts to subdue the Welsh. The discovery of Arthur's body would show that he was actually dead; and not merely sleeping, as folklore asserted, until such time as he rose and led the British (that is the Welsh) to victory. Dr Gransden concludes that the monks 'deliberately buried two skeletons, complete with inscribed cross, and then staged the discovery'; being careful to invite a well-known writer, Gerald of Wales, to view the proceedings. Following the exhumation, the bones were moved first to a chapel in the south aisle of the new church, and later to a black marble mausoleum.

A century later, the bones were again translated. Edward I, as well as being an Arthurian enthusiast, still needed to impress upon the Welsh that Arthur was dead. In 1278, he and Queen Eleanor accordingly visited Glastonbury. The tomb was opened 'and there separately in two chests painted with their images and arms, were found the bones of Arthur of wonderful size and the bones of Queen Guinevere of wonderful beauty'. Arthur's left ear had been cut off 'with the marks of the blow which slew him' visible. The next day, the king and queen wrapped the bones in precious stuffs, returned them to their chests and replaced them in the black marble mausoleum, now moved to a place in front of the high altar, seen there by Leland in the sixteenth century (p.51). The 'heads and cheeks' however were kept out 'on account of the devotion of the people', as relics.

The shrine of Arthur, as now set up, was embellished with inscriptions and imagery. The epitaph:

> *Hic jacet Arthurus flos regum, gloria regni: quem mors, probitas commendat laude perhenni.*
> Here lies Arthur, the flower of Kingship, the kingdom's glory, whom his morals and virtue commend with eternal praise.

At the head end was a cross, and at the foot of the tomb was the 'image' of Arthur, and a further inscription:

> *Arthuri jacet hic conjux tumulata secunda Que meruit celos virtutum prole seconda.*
> Arthur's fortunate wife lies buried here, who merited heaven through the happy consequences of her virtues.

There were also two lions at the head of the tomb, and two at the feet.

By the fifteenth century, it seems there was, a 'bill-board' somewhere within the monastery: a large manuscript was fixed to boards attached to a wooden frame opening like a book. This had stories of various shrines associated with the Abbey, including those of Arthur and Joseph of Arimathea.

The thirteenth-century shrine of Arthur presumably survived until the Dissolution, when it was almost totally destroyed. The base was found in excavation (see **42**). 'Arthur', however, lived on in folk memory, and remains a powerful symbol for visitors to Glastonbury to the present day, as well as for artists and writers: Tennyson's Arthur, who at his end saw himself:

> . . . going a long way . . .
> To the island-valley of Avilion;
> Where falls not hail, or rain, or any snow,
> Nor ever wind blows loudly; but it lies
> Deep-meadowed, happy, fair with orchard lawns
> And bowery hollows crowned with summer sea,
> Where I will heal me of my grievous wound.

The most recent manifestation of the belief was in 1991. This was the 800th anniversary of the 1191 exhumation; a celebration was held to commemorate the 'finding of the burial place of King Arthur and Queen Guinevere, by the monks of Glastonbury Abbey'. The advertising campaign leaflet backed up this claim by the reprinting of a newspaper article of 1963 reporting Dr Ralegh Radford's claim to have discovered the grave in his excavations of that year.

The lead cross

This small cross is one of the most discussed and illustrated objects associated with Glastonbury (**21**). Where it was found and what the inscription said were described in the later, interpolated, editions of William of Malmesbury, and by Gerald of Wales, Adam of Domerham and John of Glastonbury; but they differed significantly in their details of the inscription. The first illustration of the cross itself appeared, however, in *Britannia* by William Camden, the famous sixteenth-century antiquary; the cross was presumably available to him to study. In his first edition of 1590 the inscription is depicted in antique lettering: *HIC JACET SEPULTUS INCLITUS REX ARTURIUS IN INSULA AVALONIA* ('Here lies buried the famous King Arthur in the island of Avalon'); there is no mention of the additions described by Gerald, including Guinevere. In the 1607 and following editions, the shape of the cross is drawn out, with the positions of the letters put in, with the same words as in 1590, but with slightly different lettering. If the drawing of 1607 is full scale, the cross would have been *c*.17.5cm (6⅞in) high.

The cross itself can be traced until the late seventeenth century. It was last recorded in Glastonbury but its present location is unknown, so it is unfortunately not available for modern study. Discussion has centred on whether this cross was really 'found' in 1191 in the grave of Arthur, and if so, was it a genuine discovery of something that had been put in the grave long before 1191, or was it, as we have suggested, a blatant forgery?

The arguments for and against its authenticity revolve at least partly around the letter forms. While not those of 'Arthur's' day (in the fifth or sixth centuries AD), they could

21 *Lead cross, said to have been found in the grave of 'Arthur' in 1191, but generally believed to be a twelfth-century forgery by the monks; the object is now lost. After Camden, 1695*

be of late Saxon date. It has been suggested by Leslie Alcock that there had originally been an inscribed stone over what he considers was the (genuine) grave of Arthur. This would have read (in Roman script) HIC SEPULTUS IACET ARTURIUS – 'Here lies buried Arthur' – or something similar. When the level of the ancient cemetery was raised by Dunstan, so it is argued, this would have been destroyed. But in order that the burial place of so famous a person should not be wholly unrecorded, the monks of the tenth century, Alcock suggests, made the cross, embellishing the inscription, and put it in the grave, where it was duly found in 1191.

If, however, the cross was a forgery of the late twelfth century, the monks would have had ample access to earlier documents in their own archives, from which to copy the letter forms; and thus were able to make the cross look ancient. The letter forms may, anyway, have been more recent: an inscription on the twelfth-century tympanum in the entrance porch of nearby Stoke-sub-Hamdon has lettering that is very similar; and as Stephen Morland has pointed out, the adjective *inclitus* is not known to have been applied to Arthur before the time of Geoffrey of Monmouth, in the earlier twelfth century.

So it must be concluded that it is likely that the cross is a forgery; and that any attempts to validate it are wishful thinking by those who believe in the existence of Arthur and his connection with Glastonbury; but it must be remembered that these constitute the great majority of those who live in or visit Glastonbury.

Joseph of Arimathea, the Thorn, the Walnut and the Staff

By the late twelfth or earlier thirteenth century, Joseph had become associated with legends in which he was said to have journeyed to the West bearing the Grail. He was an appropriate figure to be named as the leader of the early missionaries who were said to have come to Glastonbury in AD 63. He was introduced as a Glastonbury figure in an interpolation to William's work in the mid-thirteenth century. By the mid-fourteenth century, the role of Joseph amongst the founders of the Abbey was fully established, together with the claim that he was buried there. An attempt to exhume his remains took place in 1345; this, and other detail about his 'grave', are discussed later in this book, in connection with mortuary practice (pp.110-112).

The first abbot seriously to promote Joseph was Chinnock. In 1382 he dedicated a chapel he had restored in the cemetery to St Michael and St Joseph. Chinnock established his claim to primacy among English abbots with the help of this promotion of the Joseph legend.

In the fifteenth century, Joseph was fully integrated into secular Arthurian literature. Sir Thomas Malory (writing 1469-70) made Joseph the ancestor of Lancelot and Galahad. Since these were concerned with the Grail, this consolidated the links between Arthur and the earlier Christian presence in the island of Glastonbury. It was also at this time that Joseph's Grail was transmuted into two cruets, containing the blood and sweat of Jesus, which later became associated with Chalice Well (p.134).

It was, however, left to Abbot Bere (abbot 1494-1525) to advance the legend to its fullest degree, establishing a shrine, and promoting Joseph to sainthood as Britain's own apostle and miracle worker; and Glastonbury as the 'holiest earth in England'. Many miraculous cures were claimed at this time.

It was also in the early sixteenth century (in a poem) that the Lady Chapel is first referred to as 'St Joseph's Chapel', its popular name today; this may then have applied only to a chapel in the sixteenth-century crypt; the name was later also attached to the Well there (p.106). The Holy Thorn (referring to the Crown of Jesus) is also first referred to in this poem:

> Thre hawthornes also, that groweth in Werall,
> Do burge and bere grene leaves at Christmas
> As freshe as other in May . . .

together with the walnut tree:

> One of the walnut trees that there doeth stande,
> In the holy ground called the semetory,
> Harde by the place where kynge Arthur was founde;
> South fro Joseph's Chapell it is walled in rounde;
> It bereth no leaves tyll the day of St Barnabè;
> And then that tree, that standeth in the grounde,
> Spreadeth his leaves as fayre as any other tree.

The Thorn became a feature for people to see when they came to Glastonbury, and to cut their initials on. One descendant was said to have been cut down by Oliver Cromwell's men to remove a focus of superstition. Others were commented on by Celia Fiennes and Daniel Defoe. Some survive today, including one in the Abbey grounds.

The Thorn is a variety of the common hawthorn, known botanically as *Crataegus monogyna*; it is recommended for winter gardens, as it does indeed flower at Christmas, as well as May, and sometimes in between. It was not, however, until the early eighteenth century that the Thorn was associated with Joseph. Travel-worn, he is said to have rested on Wirral Hill; and he exclaimed (oddly, in English), 'Friends, we are *weary all*'; and thrust his knotted staff in the ground, which burst into bloom.

There were appropriate antecedents for this miracle. St Joseph of Nazareth was known in ancient tradition by his flowering staff; and, in England, the Anglo-Saxon St Aldhelm, when he was preaching, fixed his ash staff in the ground, where it put forth boughs and leaves. More locally, the same story is attached to St Benignus. What was said to be the tomb of Joseph, previously in a shrine in the Abbey, was moved to St John's churchyard in 1665, where it can still be seen, with the initials

'JA'. The legend of St Joseph has taken root in popular imagination to an astonishing degree, extending even into the contemporary celebrations at Glastonbury by both the Anglican and Roman Churches. It has also received the ultimate accolade of being featured in a splendid British postage stamp (**colour plate 5**) and a sprig of the Thorn is sent annually to the Queen at Christmas.

No accounts of this legend make any references to the extreme difficulty of making the journey from the Holy Land to Britain in the middle of the first century AD; while such a voyage by sea is a possibility (as it was in the sixth century, p.69), the journey across southern Britain or Somerset would have been hazardous in the extreme, coinciding as it would have with the campaigns of the Roman Conquest.

The earliest church; the *vetusta ecclesia*

Some people at Glastonbury maintain that the religion of Christianity was already present there before Christ was born; and that the 'Druids' of the place were only waiting for the natal event so that the religion could be given a name!

This is the extreme case for a very early Christian centre at Glastonbury. The first description of an ancient church is in the late tenth-century *Life of Dunstan* (the 'B' *Life*):

> In that place at God's command the first neophytes of the catholic law discovered an ancient church, built by no human skill . . . consecrated to Christ and the holy Mary . . .

William of Malmesbury amplified this account, describing how the first church was built by the disciples of Christ. He was, however, cautious; while admitting that such early origins were not impossible, he comments, 'I will leave such disputable matters and stick to solid facts'. In later medieval interpolations to William's accounts, twelve disciples were sent over from Gaul, with Joseph at their head. They were each given land; these portions were identified with the 'Twelve Hides' (p.146) (12 was a favourite number in medieval writing). They built a wattle church in honour of the Blessed Mary, 31 years after the Passion and 15 years after the Assumption (i.e. in AD 63). This was the first church in the land, and it was dedicated to his mother by the Lord himself. The place was then deserted until the days of King Lucius and the missionaries sent from Rome (as recounted by Bede and the *Anglo-Saxon Chronicle*, but with no mention of Glastonbury). Bligh Bond envisaged this early church as set in a palisaded enclosure, with cells of the twelve hermits (**22**).

In his original text, William refers to the wattle church having been covered with wooden planks and roofed with lead by Paulinus (the English missionary who was Archbishop of York in 625-33; Bede relates a similar story about Paulinus elsewhere). This is the Old Church or *vetusta ecclesia* or (in Old English) *ealdechirche* (pp.89-96); William is the first known author to use the Latin expression *vetusta ecclesia*, the designation so frequently used nowadays for the earliest church.

Some modern writers offer accounts which rationalise these early origins. It is said that Joseph, who had business interests in Britain (lead or tin mining perhaps), travelled to Britain with his young nephew, Christ, thereby, (as Geoffrey Ashe comments) explaining the Bible's silence about Jesus from the age of 12 until his maturity). In this scenario, Joseph and Jesus could have founded the shrine at Glastonbury, which could thus have been dedicated by Christ himself. Other early churches, of the late Roman and post-Roman centuries, were claimed by the medieval monks, such as that of St David (see p.43).

The earliest church which can be accepted as having really existed is the *vetusta ecclesia*. As noted above, this was actually seen and described by William of Malmesbury (though presumably in a much altered form) in the earlier twelfth century, and survived until the fire of 1184. This church is unlikely to be older than the seventh century (p.92), though there were earlier buildings on the Tor in the sixth century, which may have been a hermitage complex (chapter 6).

The only crumbs of comfort which may be offered to those who would like to believe in churches at Glastonbury in the first four centuries AD are the Roman finds from the Abbey, which may include one or more wells. One of these, outside the south-east corner of the *vetusta ecclesia*, could indeed be associated with something earlier in this area (p.109).

St Patrick

The earliest reference to St Patrick at Glastonbury is in the 'B' *Life of Dunstan*; this also mentions learned Irish pilgrims, whose books Dunstan apparently studied as

22 *Imaginary reconstruction of the first Christian community in Glastonbury from a painting by Frederick Bligh Bond, done in 1939. A central church or oratory is surrounded by twelve cells for hermits, all inside a palisade*

a youth (it is not until a later date that this was amplified into there having been an Irish 'school' at Glastonbury at this time). The Irish, author 'B' recounts, had a great veneration for Glastonbury because 'the blessed Patrick is said to rest there'. Other tenth-century documents refer to Patrick being buried at Glastonbury; and it is clear that a cult of St Patrick existed at Glastonbury in the earlier tenth century. One problem is that there were two Patricks; and we do not know which may have been enshrined in the Abbey church; nor what the historical basis for this might have been. It is not until the twelfth century that there is any reference to Bridget, another Irish saint (p.148).

In the medieval period, the monks forged the so-called 'Charter of St Patrick', which was then interpolated into William's writings. This tells how Patrick came to Glastonbury after his conversion of Ireland (in the fifth century) and found certain holy men living the life of anchorites. They elected him as their superior; and subsequently Patrick and one of them went up to the Tor. They stayed here three months fasting and praying in the ruins of the old chapel (built by Phagan and Deruvian). Later it was decided that two of the brethren should always reside on the Tor and serve its chapel. The first pair to do so were two Irish companions of Patrick, Arnulph and Ogmar. This account may be compared with the archaeological evidence from the Tor described in chapter 6. The names of St Patrick's brethren as given in the 'charter' were ingeniously suggested by Watkin to be remarkably similar to those on the larger pyramid (p.42); or were they copied from that source?

Patrick is important to Glastonbury in relation to its apparent Irish connection, but which came first is difficult to ascertain; neither Patrick nor the Glastonbury Irish can be documented before the late Saxon period.

St Indracht

The third Irish saint commemorated at Glastonbury was St Indracht, reputedly buried on the north side of the altar of the Old Church. He also has some claim to have been an historical figure. There is no mention of him in the surviving written sources, however, before the second quarter of the eleventh century. A *Life* of the late eleventh or early twelfth century claimed to be based on an earlier Anglo-Saxon account, now lost, but probably of tenth-century date.

The *Life* tells how, in the late seventh or early eighth century, Indracht, the son of an Irish king, went to Rome, with nine colleagues. On their return they decided to go to Glastonbury to visit the shrine of St Patrick. There was possibly a pilgrim route across southern England at this time, from the mouth of the Parrett in the west and including Malmesbury on its line further to the east, so that Glastonbury might well have been a useful stopping place.

The pilgrims stopped for the night near Glastonbury (at Shapwick?), and were all murdered by thegns who believed they were carrying gold (in fact celery seed!).

Miraculous signs followed, and the bodies were translated, by order of King Ina, to the church at Glastonbury; further miracles followed. William of Malmesbury saw Indracht's shrine in the twelfth century. It is possible that this Indract can be equated with a later figure, named Indrechtach, who is mentioned in the Irish Annals. He was an abbot who was murdered by the English while on a trip to Rome in 854. Michael Lapidge suggests that it was he who was buried at Glastonbury in the Old Church. The monks did not, however, know anything about him except that he was a cleric; Lapidge concludes that a monk was then commissioned to write his (fictitious) *Life*, which transposed him back to the days of King Ina.

The cult of relics

Glastonbury (like many medieval churches) claimed to possess a great many relics, by which its status could be magnified. These might be actual physical remains of those who were buried at the Abbey, as described in the previous pages; or separate bones, fluids, flesh, clothing, personal possessions or other items associated with holy people.

Relics at Glastonbury might be aquired (often in good faith), donated by kings, ecclesiastics, nobles or pilgrims, or even made. The more relics an institution possessed, the more famous and ancient it could claim to be. The prestige of the owners increased, and the 'power of the saint drew pilgrims; and gave spiritual power and protection by his priviledged position in the unseen world'.

Relics were necessary in order to establish a cult, which then had to be developed, by the demonstration of miracles, or by the commissioning of a *Life*, often based on an earlier ideal model rather than entirely on fact. Relics were also useful in attracting pilgrims, who were sold badges to attach to their clothing. Two groups of surviving badges relate to the Glastonbury traditions. One group illustrates the hawthorn of St Joseph; the other, a flowery shield with a sword, illustrates the conjuction between Joseph and Arthur. A small badge of the Virgin was found on the Tor (p.82).

Patrick's remains were claimed as early as the tenth century; those of the Northumbrian St Aidan were also mentioned as being at Glastonbury in an early eleventh-century source, the *List of saints' resting places*.

A wide variety of relics are listed as having been at the Abbey. Few, if any, of these relics are likely to have been 'genuine' though many may have borne insignia of 'authentication'. This was the case everywhere: no less than a dozen foreskins of Christ were claimed as genuine in Europe.

Equally prestigious were the remains of kings; here we are on firm historical ground. Many English kings were buried at such great monastic sites; those at Glastonbury are Edmund (d.946), Edgar (d.968) and Edmund Ironside (d.1016). These graves were visited by other kings; Cnut, 'did honour to the corpse of Edmund as to a brother, with pious lamentations, and laid upon the sepulchre his cloak, which they say was woven with many-coloured peacock feathers'. The kings were also major benefactors to the Abbey, giving both land and treasure.

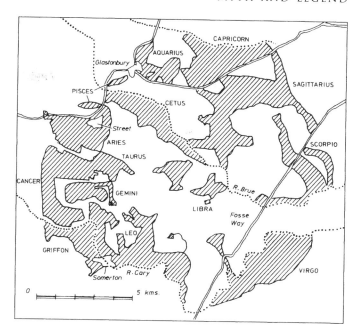

23 *The Zodiac: the shaded areas are the outlines of figures discerned by Katherine Maltwood on maps and aerial photographs of the area to the south-east of Glastonbury. She believed that these were the signs of the zodiac imprinted on the landscape in prehistoric times.* After Burrow, 1983

Few relics survived the Dissolution. A nail from the Cross remained in the possession of an old man; it was taken from him by Protestants, but the case in which it had been contains retained the nail's impression. This was seen and recorded by one Father Weston in the 1850s; he noted the nail had been a foot long.

Impressive though Glasonbury's lists of relics are, they are by no means unusual in their character or number; what is surprising is how little was made of them before the high Middle Ages in the way of evocative stories. Indeed the lack of engaging tales about Glastonbury in William of Malmesbury's general histories is most striking – there is nothing to rival the miracle of Birstan, Bishop of Winchester; when he sang psalms in the churchyard at night for the souls of the dead, they responded. Nor like the memorable anecdote about Etheldreda, a seventh-century saint of Ely. Her tomb was desecrated by a Dane; when subsequently, during an attempt to ascertain whether her body was incorrupt, her clothes were pulled through the hole left by the Dane, she indignantly pulled them back and the perpetrator of this deed was duly punished.

Relics were nevertheless a fundamental feature of the Abbey as a monastic institution. As John of Glastonbury comments: 'there is no path through the church or cemetery which is free from the ashes of the blessed.'

The Zodiac

The final 'myth' to be considered is really an archaeological one, of cosmic dimensions: the Glastonbury Zodiac (**23**). This is a pattern seen on maps and air photographs that is claimed to be a representation on the ground of the celestial figures in the stars. Katherine Maltwood (1878-1961) was a sculptress and book illustrator. In the 1930s she was illustrating an edition of *The High History of the Holy Grail*. In looking for topographical clues on maps she believed she could see the Zodiac figures: gigantic 'effigies' in an area some 16km (10 miles) in diameter, related to the medieval mysteries of the quest for the Grail. She dated their delineation to the Neolithic period – the third or fourth millennium BC. Her theory was backed up by lavish publications of both maps and air photographs, and has gained considerable credence among Arthurian enthusiasts and Glastonbury disciples.

There are, however, serious objections to the idea of such a 'Temple of the Stars' even if the shapes delineated were more convincing representations of the Zodiac figures. The most pertinent reservations concern the criteria by which the boundaries of each figure are defined. They are varied: some could be ancient, such as the courses of rivers, streams or old trackways; but they also include field boundaries, drainage channels, turnpike roads and droveways, which can be dated historically to the last few hundred years. Leo's foreleg, for instance, is formed by a diversion of the road for a new railway in 1905. The eye of Capricorn is a haystack stand. The eye of one of the Pisces on Wirrall Hill is a morass caused by cows trampling the area around a field gate. In fairness to Mrs Maltwood, she would say that all these modern features unconsciously perpetrated ancient markings through folk memory. Certain place names were also cited in support: Wagg in the sign of Canis (the Dog), or Fish Lane by one of the Pisces (the Fishes).

As long ago as 1935, the great field archaeologist O.G.S. Crawford pointed out the problems, and suggested that similar figures could be drawn out using almost any set of Ordnance Survey maps and a pair of scissors. Belief in the Zodiac, like that in ley-lines and many other features in this chapter, is a matter of faith rather than reason.

When Mrs Maltwood died, she left a considerable sum of money to further the understanding of her ideas. The Trust which administers this has taken the liberal view that understanding of the Zodiac will be achieved only by a wider understanding of the archaeology of Somerset; to this end many grants have been made to archaeologists in the area (including the present authors), for which we must be thankful.

Conclusion

The mythical figures and stories of Glastonbury, whatever their origin, have long been part of the fabric of the place. The early printing of the Abbey chronicles meant that these and especially the supposed association of Arthur and the 'Celtic' saints continued to be available. Glastonbury thus gained a special place in both popular history and in Arthurian literature. The extravagant 'origin myths' of other abbeys were in contrast often lost sight of. It is on to these foundations that the modern myths of Glastonbury have been grafted.

6

GLASTONBURY TOR

The Tor (**colour plate 1**) is the most remarkable of several prominent hills in this area of Somerset. It can be seen for up to 40km (25 miles) from all directions, and must always have been a major landmark, dominating the whole of Glastonbury peninsula; it is especially striking from the Levels to the south and west. It rises to a height of over 150m (500ft) (**colour plate 3**), and its sides are precipitous. Its geology and the reason for its prominence have been discussed in chapter 2. The softness of the Lias strata below the sandstone capping does give rise to consider-able instability and landslips, and vulnerability to earthquakes. This instability must always have made any building on the summit rather insecure.

In prehistoric times the Tor would have been a major landmark to all dwellers in the area and to travellers, making Glastonbury easy to find. Buildings on it would have been highly visible. Of the later churches to be discussed, only the tower now survives, and this gives an even sharper 'point' to the Tor for visitors of recent centuries.

The sides of the Tor are prominently terraced (**colour plate 1**). There are two usual explanations for this, which may be complementary. The first is that the terraces are the result of natural differential erosion of the numerous layers of stone and clay which comprise the Lias mass. The second, perhaps taking advantage of the first, is that the terraces are strip lynchets, platforms for ploughing, deliber-ately created to extend the areas of arable cultivation in the land-hungry times of the Middle Ages or to grow vines. These terraces extend the familiar ridge and furrow cultivation of the flatter land up on to steeper slopes (well illustrated by Dugdale (**25**)).

While these functional explanations are probably true, it is worth mentioning a much more dramatic interpretation put forward by the late Geoffrey Russell in the 1960s. He believed that the Tor slopes had been engineered into a gigantic three-dimensional maze (**26**), of the classic pattern best known from its delinea-tion in the floor of the cathedral at Chartres. He made a series of sand-models which were quite convincing in relating the earthworks to the maze plan; and in 1964 he commissioned an aerial photogrammetric survey, with contours at

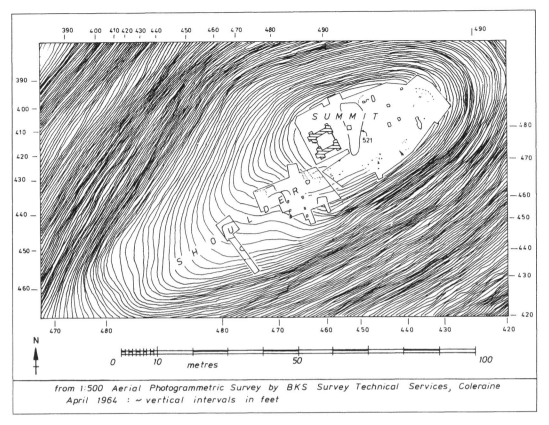

24 *Contour survey of Glastonbury Tor; this shows the steepness of the slopes, with a slightly easier ascent from the south-west. Dark Age, Anglo-Saxon and medieval structures were erected on the upper part of the easier slope (the shoulder) and on the flatter summit. PAR, 1989*

intervals of 1ft (**24**). From this a more thorough testing of his hypothesis could, he hoped, be carried out; and the truth about the terraces could of course be shown by excavation.

If he was right, such a major work could only be early prehistoric, of the Neolithic period, in the third or second millennium BC; engineering skill at this time is well attested by the great earth and stone moving operations of the henges, such as Avebury. The maze would have been a major cultural and religious focus for the area, initiating the fame of Glastonbury in later times. It is at least more credible than the 'Zodiac' discussed in chapter 5.

A less likely story occurs in the medieval life of St Collen. This describes how the saint came to Glastonbury, and quarrelled with the monks. He left for the 'mountain of Glastonbury', and made a cell in a quiet spot near a rock. He had a curious vision of the King of the Underworld (Gwyn ap Nudd). He sprinkled holy water, and the vision (which included a castle, musicians and dishes of dainties), vanished, leaving only 'green tumps'.

The Tor has featured recently in the more extremist beliefs concerning Glastonbury (chapter 10). Some believe it to be hollow, still the resort of fairies and other underworld lifeforms; or that it is a great cone of energy and life-force. What is true is that it has been (and probably still is) a focus for witchcraft. If such associations were of ancient origin, or if the maze theory is true, it might explain the Christian interest in the area: an evil to be fought and overcome, even on the Tor itself.

The Chalice Well Trust, through its Chairman, the late Major Wellesley Tudor Pole, and with the backing of the Russell Trust and American sponsors, commissioned three seasons of excavations on the Tor, in 1964-6, following that at Chalice Well (p.134). It was hoped that such work might throw light on the Christian origins of Glastonbury; and that important finds might be made, especially concerning the legendary associations of the time of Christ, in the first century AD.

Although the dig was very rewarding in academic archaeological terms, the results were not those that the sponsors or their followers might have hoped for. Indeed, one lady visitor said it was not surprising that 'nothing had been found' for three reasons: firstly, the excavation was in the wrong place, secondly, it was being done at the wrong 'time' and thirdly, it was being directed by the wrong person (PAR).

Excavations 1964-6

The work on the Tor was arduous. All tools and surveying gear had to be carried up each day; the wind was ferocious and blew the soil back in the diggers' faces; when it was fine, it was like an oven. Added to this, the fissured bedrock (see **32**) made recognition of features difficult; and erosion and medieval building had removed much of the earlier levels.

25 *Drawing of the Tor by William Dugdale (c.1670). He shows field systems of medieval date extending part way up the slopes, but above these only terraces.* From Carley, 1981

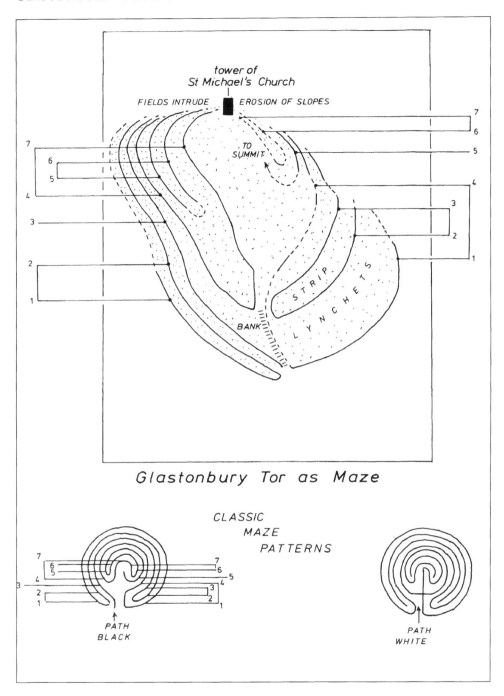

26 *The maze on the Tor as envisaged by Geoffrey Russell in 1971. He believed that the terraces on the slopes were originally a three-dimensional maze, based on the classic maze pattern as seen in many places in Europe. After G.N. Russell, 1971*

The earliest finds were flints of Upper Palaeolithic, Neolithic and later date (c.10,000-1000 BC); there was also a Neolithic polished axe, of a greenish stone not found locally (see **9**). These finds do not necessarily imply that anyone was living on the Tor in prehistoric times; rather that there were occasional visits over a long period of time, for reasons which can only be guessed at, unless the prehistoric maze discussed above is thought credible.

There were also Roman finds – pottery and tile; some of the metal objects found may also have been of this date. Although these finds are Roman in their date of manufacture, they may have survived to be used in the post-Roman settlement that followed.

The Dark Age settlement

The discoveries of major importance were, however, of the fifth to seventh centuries AD – probably in the case under discussion, the sixth. Although the flattest part of the summit had been heavily disturbed by the medieval church (see **37**), intact layers survived on the sides of the summit, where the bedrock slopes gently away before the precipitous down slopes begin (except to the west).

It was in these layers that sherds of Dark Age date were found. Most of these were of amphorae (**27**); these are storage or transit vessels used in antiquity for wine, olive oil, fish sauce and a wide variety of other materials. They were imported from the Mediterranean, and can be matched there from dated fifth- or sixth-century levels. These imports are fundamental in the west of England in the identification of Dark Age sites. Since the Roman coin supply to Britain had dried up by that time, and very little ordinary pottery was being made, they are virtually the only datable material (apart from organic material suitable for radiocarbon dating). They have been found at other places in Somerset, in Devon and Cornwall, and in Wales (**28**). There has been much discussion about the mechanism by which they got to Britain. Whoever it was who brought them, this long sea voyage was presumably bringing not only wine or olive oil, but also other low bulk, high-value materials such as spices or silk from the far east. Merchants would be hoping to exchange these for whatever British people could provide – notably gold, silver, tin, hunting dogs, furs or slaves. It is generally agreed that those participating in this trade in Britain were people of some importance such as local kings or chiefs, or ecclesiastical dignitaries. The other find-spots in western Britain are mostly defended hillforts, but there are also a few sherds from possible early monastic sites. In their countries of origin, the population was by this time mostly Christian, and indeed some sherds of table-ware (not found on the Tor) carry Christian symbols. So this is one mechanism whereby Christian ideas and perhaps even missionaries could have found their way into the western parts of Britain, before the arrival of Augustine at the court of Kent at the end of the sixth century.

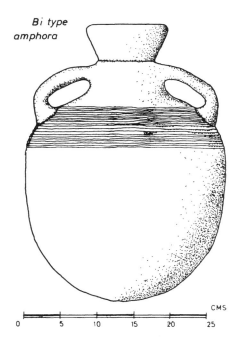

Bi type
amphora

CMS

0   5   10   15   20   25

27 *Amphora of the sixth century, from the East Mediterranean, used for the shipment of wine, olive oil and other liquids; sherds of such vessels were found in the Dark Age settlement on Glastonbury Tor and at the Mound*

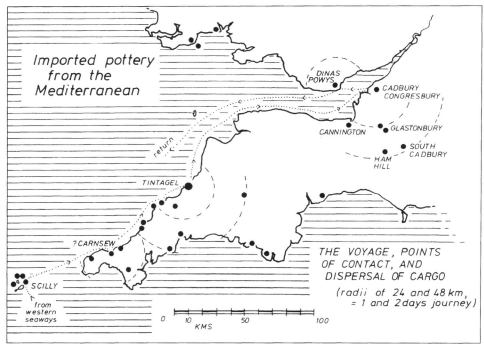

28 *Map of the final stages of the voyage of a ship carrying amphorae and other goods from the Mediterranean to the Bristol Channel area. Charles Thomas has suggested that the small amounts of material found at the places shown were the result of visits to successive ports, and the diffusion from these to places further inland.* After Thomas 1991

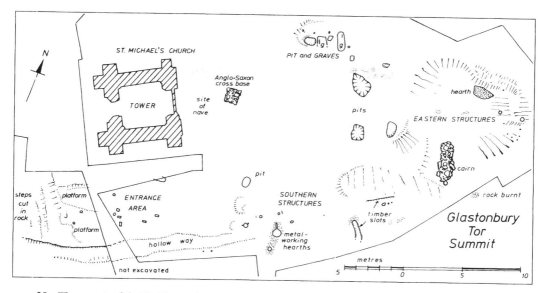

29 *The summit of the Tor. The Dark Age settlement is shown here, together with the Anglo-Saxon cross base and the tower of the medieval church; the nave of this was to the north-east of the tower; its construction will have destroyed any earlier features in this area.* PAR, 1971

Also found were a great many animal bones, mostly of cattle, but with a few of sheep and pig. These are the residues of joints brought to the site, from animals already butchered elsewhere. The areas of Dark Age settlement on the summit of the Tor are shown in **29**, in relation to the tower of St Michael's Church which survives today. The finds discussed above were associated with a series of timber structures; these were indicated by cuts in the rock for upright posts and sill-beams (timber slots), and by hearths, hollows and pits.

On the north side of the later church was a small structure indicated by post-holes; and a (?latrine) pit, with an area of burnt rock on its north-west side (**30**). Close by were two graves with enough of the leg-bones surviving to show 'that the graves were orientated south-north, with heads to the south. The bones were of young people, well under twenty years old; but it was not possible to determine their sex. This might have been a small hermitage, with the graves of two hermits. Such an interpretation is possible; but the graves would in this case be more likely to be west-east in the manner that came to be adopted by Christians.

Oddly enough, there is a mention of 'two lay brothers' on the Tor, named Arnulph and Ogmar. This is in the famous 'charter of St Patrick' (p.62), a medieval forgery, purporting to refer to the time of St Patrick in the late fourth to early fifth centuries. While this cannot be taken as historical evidence, it does suggest that there was a medieval tradition that there was a monastic foundation on the Tor in early times, with two hermits.

At the east end there were more post- and stake-holes, belonging to one or more structures; burnt rock areas; and a large hearth – a hollow with charcoal and

30 *Pit, post-holes and graves on the north side of the summit of the Tor; other stones and cuts visible are related to the later church. Viewed from the west*

burnt animal bone. On the south side there was a remarkable cairn aligned north-south, of local stones (**31**). It was hoped that this might cover an important grave, but there was only an iron ferrule (of Roman or Dark Age date) under it, and a patch of woodash.

To the west was the entrance complex. The summit was reached from the 'shoulder' to the west by crude shallow steps cut in the rock; and by a hollow way skirting the south side. At the top of the steps were two platforms cut in the rock, with post-holes and timber-slots – perhaps there were small structures here.

The southern structures are the most interesting. In a wide platform cut into the rock were post-holes and timber-slots, and hollows indicating more structures at the end of the hollow way. There were also two burnt hearth hollows (**32**). These were metalworking hearths, using bellows and tuyères (clay nozzles for directing the air-blast). Close by were two small crucible fragments (**33**) with residues of greenish copper alloy slags.

Near these was found a remarkable head (**33**), possibly a product of this workshop. This consists of a 'mask' of bronze – a hollow casting fitted over an iron core. It is part of a larger object, such as the escutcheon of a pail handle, or possibly from the head of a bishop's crozier. The head has a long narrow 'Celtic' face. The eyes are hollow, and may have been filled with enamel. The upper part is covered by a domed helmet, with heavy ridges above the eyes, and ear flaps.

The structures and finds of Dark Age date are earlier than anything found in the Abbey. The nature of this settlement is, however, debatable. The buildings were on a spot likely to be chosen for reasons other than the normal ones. There

31 *The cairn at the east end of the summit of the Tor, from the south-west*

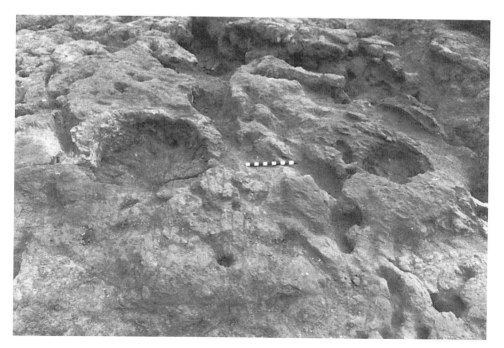

32 *Metalworking hearth hollows cut in the rock on the south side of the Tor summit, from the west*

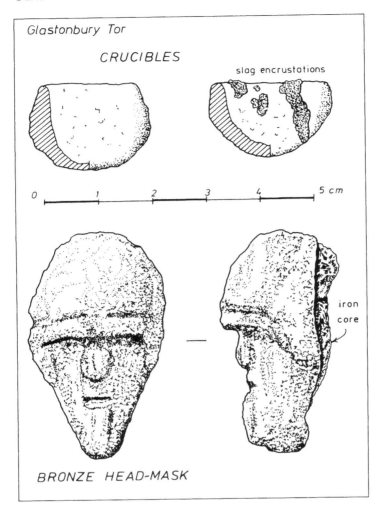

33 *Finds from the Dark Age settlement on the Tor: crucibles for metalworking, and a bronze head-mask, from the escutcheon of a pail-handle or a crozier.* PAR, 1991

is no water (though the Chalice Well spring (**colour plate 6**) provides ample supplies at the foot of the hill). The Tor summit is remote, inaccessible, inconvenient and very exposed; but does have an excellent view!

To summarise, the buildings were of timber, set in platforms cut in the rock. The inhabitants ate high quality prepared meat. They had access to imported Mediterranean amphorae and perhaps drank wine or used olive oil from these; craft-workers produced small-scale, high-class craftwork in metal.

Two principal explanations for this evidence may be postulated: one is related to security, defence and prestige; the other to religious motivation. The second can be further subdivided into pagan and Christian. The secular aspects will be considered first.

In the time of the decline and collapse of Roman administration, in the late fourth and fifth centuries AD, local leaders set up defensive strongholds, and society reverted to some extent to Iron Age patterns, of local chiefs or petty kings ruling fairly small areas. In most of Britain, this went on for two or three centuries, before the Anglo-Saxons achieved dominance and developed their own kingdoms.

Such local strongholds were often reused and refortified Iron Age hillforts; notable examples in Somerset are the two Cadburys, at South Cadbury (south of Glastonbury) and Cadbury Congresbury, near the coast of the British Channel. At both of these sites, Mediterranean imparted pottery has been found, similar to that on the Tor (see **28**). Such local elites were able to participate in the international trade discussed above.

Glastonbury Tor could be another such stronghold, its steep slopes providing the same security as the earthwork defences of a hillfort. A local ruler here could dominate at least the peninsula, if not also parts of the rich marshy areas of the Somerset Levels nearby.

A late medieval source in fact names such a person — Melwas. In legend, he abducted Guinevere and kept her in his eyrie-like stronghold. Arthur besieged him for a long time, but the natural defences of hill, marsh and river were too strong. Peace was mediated by Gildas, then a monk at the Abbey. While this cannot be taken as true history, it is in keeping with the scenario suggested above.

Such a ruler would have several buildings on the Tor, slight though they might seem from the archaeological evidence; he or she would be powerful enough to command the same resources and wealth as chiefs in hillforts.

The religious interpretation would, in a pagan guise, see the activity an the Tor as associated with a local Roman temple or, more probably, a shrine, surviving into post-Roman times. Such hilltop structures are numerous in Somerset (see p.32); there are examples at nearby Priest's Hill, Pedwell; Lamyatt Beacon; and probably South Cadbury. Some such sites were adapted for Christian use in post-Roman times and this could have happened on the Tor. A wholly Christian interpretation would envisage the Tor as the abode of hermits, for whom the remoteness and inaccessibility of the hilltop would be an advantage, comparable to seclusion on islands or marshy places, imitating desert monasteries of the early Fathers in Egypt. Such places might also participate in the distribution of imported luxuries, perhaps through aristocratic patronage. Wine could be used in the mass; and as noted above, the pottery links were potentially also those of early Christian evangelists or 'saints'.

When the results of the excavations were published in 1971, a secular/pagan interpretation was suggested for two principal reasons: firstly, the un-Christian orientation of the two apparently associated graves; and secondly, and more importantly, the evidence of considerable meat-eating of prime cuts. These did not at the time seem to be consistent with Christian affiliations or with an ascetic life-style. Since 1971 the significance of the presence of the bones has been rather undermined by the finding of extensive evidence for meat-eating at no less holy a place than Iona, and also recently at Whithorn. It seems probable that traditional views of ascetic early monasticism in western Britain have been based on written sources rather than archaeological evidence. It is thus possible that Glastonbury Tor was, in the later fifth or early sixth century, a monastic site; and if so, one of the earliest in Britain.

This monastic interpretation is now preferred; influenced also by the fact that the Anglo-Saxon development of the Tor (below) was certainly monastic, and that the site became an important adjunct to the Abbey itself in later centuries.

The Tor was, it is suggested, the pre-Saxon religious nucleus of Glastonbury, of such repute ultimately that it attracted major support from the incoming Anglo-Saxon rulers of Wessex; that the inconvenience of access to the Tor and its restricted space necessitated expansion to a new site. This was found in the flatter area where the Abbey now stands.

An alternative scenario would combine both secular and Christian elements: that the Tor was a secular stronghold of a local 'king', with his own territory; and that (as was often the case) he was visited by missionaries who sought both to convert him and his court, and to obtain permission to preach and convert in his area. This was successful and established an important Christian nucleus in the vicinity, similarly developed in later decades.

The Anglo-Saxon monastery on the Tor

The Dark Age settlement was succeeded by an Anglo-Saxon monastery (**colour plate 7**). It is not known whether there is continuity between the Dark Age occupation and that which followed. There may well have been a gap in time between the decline of Dark Age political and social systems and the full establishment of Anglo-Saxon control over both church and state in the late seventh or eighth centuries, now on a sound Christian basis. The new order led to a major expansion of the faith at Glastonbury, which found its expression in the Abbey site. The earliest features there are assigned to the seventh century, but with the possibility of a British foundation before a fully Anglo-Saxon one.

Anything on the Tor in the Anglo-Saxon period must be seen as subsidiary to the Abbey: a daughter settlement or hermitage, with others such as Beckery to be described later. If our interpretation of this period is correct, a tradition of eremitic isolation may be envisaged, continuing or renewed after a gap.

On the summit, the only structure that can be assigned to the Anglo-Saxon period is a squarish foundation (**34**), orientated on the compass points (unlike the churches which succeeded it); this is interpreted as the base for a standing cross. The head of a wheel-cross, found just below the summit, may be the upper part of this. It is broken off at the base from a plinth. The possible size of this is shown in **35**, making a standing cross c.1.55m (5ft) high. This is about the height of a person, enough to be visible on the summit from some distance; it would have been mortared on to the foundation discovered. The cross is dated to the tenth or eleventh century, probably before the Conquest.

The principal structures lay on the 'shoulder' of the Tor (see **34** & **36**), a flattish area below the summit on the west side, which breaks the otherwise precipitous slopes. The biggest structure, indicated by large post-pits, was thought to be a timber church (*c*.5.5 by 4.2m, 18 by 14ft), though its north-south orientation makes this questionable; a communal building is perhaps as likely. It was approached by a series of platforms from the west, which possibly held other or earlier structures (p.108). To the north were hearths and a deep pit, possibly lined to hold water; and a fence emplacement bounded the east side. Beyond this, east of the church or communal building, was a squarish area, deeply cut into the rock, with post-holes and a possible 'verandah' to a terrace to the south. This is interpreted as a monastic cell, half underground, with a timber superstructure; it was well-protected from the prevailing winds, and had a pleasant aspect to the south.

Another larger but similar cell, was found further west (**36**), with some post-holes and fragments of stone walling. A more extensive terrace lay to the south of this, with a pit and post-holes, and a burnt floor; this was bounded by a timber wall.

The cross-head is the earliest certainly Christian find from the Tor; but a monastic use for the other structures is supported both by aspects of their plan, and by the food remains: those of this phase comprise bird bones (goose, domestic fowl, stock dove and corncrake); fish (pike, perch, rudd, coalfish, hake and cod); eggshells; but only eleven bones of sheep or cattle, in contrast to the food remains of Dark Age date.

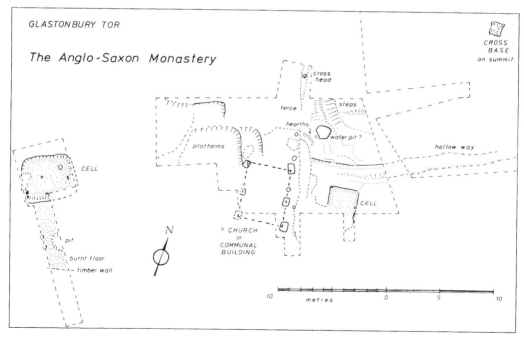

34 *Plan of the Anglo-Saxon monastery on the shoulder of the Tor; only selected areas were excavated.* After Rahtz, 1971

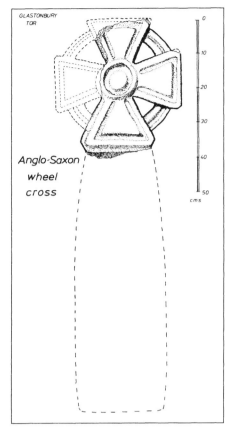

35 *Reconstruction of a wheel-cross from the Anglo-Saxon monastery on the Tor.* PAR, 1991

This monastic settlement may have served as a hermitage or retreat for monks at the Abbey; it appears to have continued into the post-Conquest period, when the importance of the Tor found its final expression in a stone church, the tower of which survives to the present day as a notable landmark.

The church of St Michael and associated buildings

The dedication, to St Michael the Archangel, is one frequently found at hilltop churches; St Michael's Mount in Cornwall, and Mont St Michel, in Brittany, are familiar examples. St Michael dedications are widespread in Britain; they are dense in Somerset. The hilltop associations are attributed to St Michael's activities in the heavens, and the elevated sites of his Visions.

> In the year of Grace 1275 on 11 September, there was a general earthquake between the first and the third hour of the day, by which the church of St Michael outside Glastonbury, which is called the Mount [de Monte] fell flattened to the ground.

Thus recorded a medieval writer; and some aspect of building or repair at this time could be related to this. The archaeological evidence is very difficult to interpret. Although the limits of the church are reasonably certain, there are formidable difficulties in interpretation. There is severe fissuring of rock (the result of land slippage or earthquake) and these fissures have been blocked by the builders with stones, which were difficult to distinguish from foundations. There has been extensive stone-robbing in later centuries and severe erosion in the tower area. There is a post-medieval grave and other modern disturbances by treasure-hunters.

The remains (**37–38**) are interpreted as representing two main phases, although this may strain the reader's credulity. The earlier we would date to the twelfth or thirteenth century. There are some pieces of worked stone of Romanesque style (including a chevron moulding), so it seems likely that parts were as early as the twelfth century; but there are thirteenth-century pieces as well.

The second church was built half a century after the earthquake, by Abbot Adam of Sodbury (1323-34). This was built of the local sandstone, with Lias and Doulting limestone. Freestone elements were of Doulting, painted white; the main walls were rendered in stucco. There were leaded windows with decorated glass, and floors of plain and decorated tiles. Finds were few, but included a fragment of a small portable altar of Purbeck marble from Dorset. This would have been used by a monk coming to say Mass at times when there was no permanent staff.

36 *The western cell of the Anglo-Saxon monastery, from the north*

The surviving tower has lost its top storey, but in the rest there are both four-teenth- and fifteenth-century architectural features. The west side, visible from the main approach, is more decorated. To the left and right of the doorway are relief panels depicting a woman milking a cow (possibly St Bridget - see p.148) and St Michael holding the scales. Three niches originally held effigies, but only in one does a headless image survive.

There was an entrance to the earlier church in the north side of its nave. This position, where the slopes are very steep, is rather puzzling, but there may have been later erosion or crumbling here. The subsequent entrance was a paved one, leading into the west side of the tower. This provided access from the area below.

Access to the buildings on the shoulder was probably on the shallowest gradient from the west afforded by the 'spine' of the Tor, where the principal modern path is set. There seems to have been at least one substantial range with stone foundations, more than 250m² (2700ft²) in area. The eastern part may have been a kitchen or bakehouse. The buildings (**colour plate 8**) had glazed windows and floors of plain and decorated tiles.

Such an extensive complex was by the later Middle Ages clearly more than just a shelter or priest's house for an isolated hilltop chapel. It implies either a substan-tial daughter-house of the Abbey; or a complex which could minister to the needs of pilgrims honouring the cult of St Michael. Another chapel to the saint was in the cemetery of the Abbey (p.109); it may be that the Abbey gained substantial

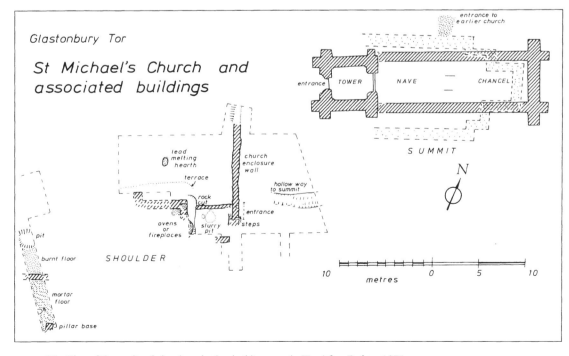

37   *Plan of the medieval church and other buildings on the Tor. After Rahtz, 1971*

38 *The tower of St Michael in the eighteenth century, in a ruinous state; from a contemporary drawing*

revenues from fostering the cult in both places, taking full advantage of the obvious attraction of the Tor as a destination of pilgrimage, as it is today. One of the finds from the excavation was a small pilgrim's badge of the Virgin and Child, appropriate to the principal cult of St Mary in the Abbey.

Some support for the Tor complex having been a daughter-house is provided by a reference to the 'monastery of St Michael on the Tor' in a charter of Henry III, of 1243. This gives permission for holding an annual six-day fair there.

Beyond the shoulder buildings to the west was a boundary wall. There was an entrance through this and steps which led up the slope to the church; access to this was either obliquely to the entrance in the west side of the tower or perhaps up the hollow way or steps discussed above in an earlier context (p.80); or even (before 1275) around the west side of the church to its northern entrance.

The end of St Michael's church and subsequent activities

The complex on the Tor shared the fate of the Abbey at the Dissolution. Indeed it was the scene of the final terrible act of that desecration – the hanging, with two other monks, of the last Abbot, Richard Whiting, who was dragged up the slopes on a hurdle (p.50). Three gallows were set up – some of the post-holes found in excavation may have been of these.

By the eighteenth century the nave of the church had been destroyed and its building materials robbed out – only the damaged tower remained, with some

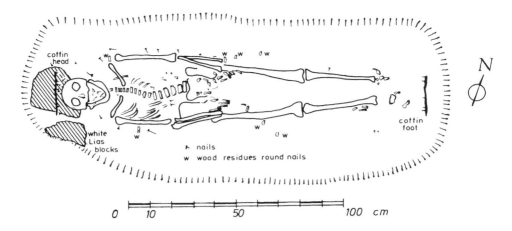

39 *The grave of John Rawls. His burial on the Tor in 1741 is recorded in the register of St John's Church.* After Watts 1967

stubs of nave walling (**38**). The church must have been in this state when the third and last burial was made, that of John Rawls, on 28 December 1741; his burial there is recorded in the burial register of St John's Church, in the town (p.128). No explanation is offered for his burial on the Tor; perhaps it was at his own request. His grave was found in the excavations at the east end (**39**). Oddly enough it was orientated on the line of the earlier of the two churches. Two Lias blocks were laid beneath the head of his coffin. This was of wood with iron nails and head and foot bars. He was left to lie there in peace, the sole custodian of the hill.

Pilgrim activity continued, both of Christian and other faiths. There are also more sinister manifestations of witchcraft (numerous pins were found in deep disturbances made by treasure-seekers). Near the tower was a gold and millefiori cross, made in Italy; and a silver ring of an eastern faith. More secular events represented by archaeological finds include the setting up of a beacon, perhaps to warn of Napoleonic invasion or to celebrate Queen Victoria's Jubilee; a lightning conductor; an Ordnance Survey trigonometrical point; and a concrete structure at the east end. This was for the use of the builders in successive tower restorations, notably in the nineteenth century, and in 1948. On this last occasion, a trolley was made with one end much higher than the other, so that the body was more or less level when the wheels were on a very steep slope. A rope was attached to this end and passed over the pulleys on the concrete structure. The other end was attached to a horse, which walked down one side of the Tor, thus pulling the cart on the other side up the slope.

The Tor is now in the care of the National Trust. In recent years the number of tourists climbing the Tor, a magnet for pilgrims of all persuasions, has increased enormously. This has caused 'visitor erosion' on both the slopes and summit. There are now concrete paths and wooden steps up to each end. These have protected the Tor from slow disintegration, but have rather detracted from the wildness of the spot, and from the challenge of climbing it.

7

THE ABBEY
AND ITS PRECINCT

The Abbey of Glastonbury does not have that choice situation which
the generality of religious houses possess

W. Gilpin, 1798

The interpretation of the documentary evidence, with reference to its
application to the buildings, is still enveloped in indecision and conjecture

Robert Willis, 1866

Introduction

In chapter 4 the dismemberment of the Abbey in the years following the
Dissolution was described. These depredations were largely at an end by the early
nineteenth century (**40**). After this the owners were more sympathetic to the
ruins, as antiquarian interests flourished in England. Little was done, however, to
consolidate or conserve the parts that were left. The natural processes of wind, frost
and rain weathering, together with damage done by vegetation, continued slowly,
and indeed, as with all ancient buildings, continue today; they are now, however,
accelerated by air pollution.

Serious historical and archaeological enquiry began in the early nineteenth
century with the work of Richard Warner. Like many later scholars who worked
on the Abbey, his interests were primarily historical and architectural, and not
archaeological as we would understand that word today. The same was true of the
seminal study of Robert Willis later in the nineteenth century, one of the greatest
of the founders of modern architectural studies of English ecclesiastical buildings.

These studies were done with the collaboration of the private owners of the site.
The last of these was Stanley Austin; but in 1907 he decided to sell. Ernest Jardine, a
wealthy industrialist, bought the Abbey for £30,000. It is said that the other principal
bidder, a wealthy American lady, wished to establish a 'school of chivalry' there, but
was thwarted by missing a train connection on the day of the auction.

A sensation ensued when it was revealed that Jardine had not bought it for
himself, but as a holding agent for the Church of England, who soon raised
the money to pay him back. There were also political undertones: in the 1906

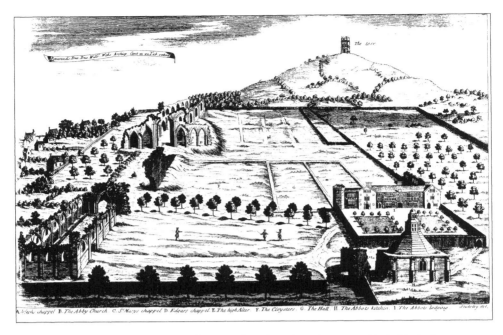

40 *William Stukeley's drawing of the Abbey grounds in the eighteenth century, with the Tor in the background. It provides a useful guide to what was visible in his day, though it cannot be relied on in detail*

election, the area had a Liberal MP. Jardine was a prospective Conservative candidate; he moved into the Abbey House and won the seat in 1910, by a large majority! The whole affair caused considerable offence to the Roman Catholic Church. It not surprisingly believed that it had a prior right to the site, which had been wrested from it at the Dissolution.

The site was at least now safe from further depredation, except by archaeologists. As seen today, it is a vast area neatly grassed. There are still some impressive fragments of the church complex standing to a considerable height (**colour plates 10 & 11**). A series of foundations and other features exposed by excavation are set out and labelled.

The area purchased did not include the built-up townscape around it. The approach to the great complex is not attractive. When Nikolaus Pevsner visited the site in the 1950s, he was appalled: '[the ruins] are a sight to be cherished by any sensitive or indeed sensible community. What meets the eye instead? Between the street and the venerable remains is the chief car park. A notice says, "To the Abbey ruins 50 yds", another next to it "Parking fees, Cars 6d, Coaches 7s", boards with notices reading "Filling Station", "Snack Bar", "Gentlemen'and 'Ladies".' Some efforts have been made in recent years to make the entry to the grounds more salubrious, through a separate entrance.

The Church Trustees could have preserved the site intact, and concentrated on conservation of above-ground remains. They might have commissioned detailed topographic and architectural surveys. This would at that time have been a relatively simple affair, compared with what could be brought to bear today: a whole armoury of modern remote sensing devices. Such techniques (excepting the architectural survey) were not available then; nor was there indeed the recognition that excavation is irreversible destruction. However carefully the work is recorded, much is lost. Each generation can get more information out of a dig than its predecessor, thanks to methodological and especially scientific advances.

The only archaeological excavation up to the time of the sale had been trenches dug by St John Hope in 1904; ten of them in one week! The Church Trustees, however, decided to sponsor work on a bigger scale; the problems of these will now be considered.

Excavations 1908–79

Thirty-four seasons of digging took place in the years 1908-79, on low budgets gathered by subscription. The work was under the joint auspices of the Society of Antiquaries of London and the Somerset Archaeological Society. The extent of ground explored is shown in **41**, involving over half of the principal church complex and monastic buildings.

A number of different directors were in charge of the work during this half century. All had broadly the same aims: to conserve the ruins; to recover the architectural and archaeological sequence from the times of the earliest Abbey to the Dissolution; and to relate this to the extensive written sources discussed earlier in the book. These aims have not however been realised. Much of the work remains unpublished except in interim reports, and there is not even an accurate overall plan of the site or the areas dug. The plan of Roger Leech (see **41**) is the best attempt so far. To compile this, he used not the plans published by the excavators (which he found inaccurate), but those of the Ordnance Survey. On to this he superimposed what he could from excavation reports, but in many cases this could only be approximate. As the reader will quickly discover, there are many inconsistencies and contradictions about the location of walls and features.

The Trustees' first Director, from 1908 to 1922, was F. Bligh Bond, a noted architect. He uncovered many parts of the medieval buildings at foundation level, and published detailed reports. These are quite up to the standards current in his day; they include many stone-by-stone drawings (see **53**) (a practice not subsequently followed up at the Abbey), and details of numerous underground drains and culverts. The latter have never been collated to provide some idea of the drainage and water systems of the Abbey.

Unfortunately, in spite of these promising beginnings, Bond, became obsessed by non-scientific theories, concerned with geometry and numbers, which led him to falsify the measurements, and postulate elements of the structure which had never existed (such as the apse of the Edgar Chapel). Worse than this, as the work proceeded, he claimed to be guided by automatic writing and spirits, notably by that of a medieval monk Johannes Bryant (1497-1533), but also including those of a clockmaker, a mason and a cowherd. This, and some decline in the quality of work, led to his dismissal in 1922 – a considerable scandal; the Church of England 'did not like the Devil to advise on Church property'! He was even made to pay for admission to the Abbey grounds in later years, as a member of the public. In 1926 he went to America, where he lectured on Glastonbury, and on his psychic techniques concerning the 'Company of Avalon'. He returned to England in 1936, and died, very much alone, in North Wales in 1945.

The excavators in the later 1920s and 1930s were also prominent architectural historians. During these years, the foundations of earlier churches were excavated, including those attributed to King Ina, of the early eighth century, and those of Abbot Dunstan.

After a break during the Second World War, further excavations (1951-63) were undertaken by Dr C.A. Ralegh Radford. He was a considerable authority on a very wide range of historical, architectural and archaeological topics, with a profound knowledge of the buildings of the Christian church in Britain and Europe. He had known Bond and visited the excavations as early as 1910 (when he was only eight or nine) and throughout the 1920s and 1930s. His especial interest was in the earliest Saxon and possible pre-Saxon remains; his interpretations were very much determined by his knowledge of both the medieval chronicles of the Abbey and also of the more general history of the Christian church. Two final seasons of digging were directed by the late W.J. ('Bill') Wedlake in 1978 and 1979, but no record of these has appeared. In these eight decades of excavation, a considerable part of the Abbey nucleus was explored, though not all areas were dug down to the undisturbed natural clay (**41**).

An attempt may now be made to summarise what has been found in the Abbey excavations, concentrating on the earliest periods, of the seventh to tenth centuries AD (**43-44**).

We begin with the most important features: the churches themselves. They formed a string extending from west to east. This eventually reached a total length of nearly 200m (660ft). Also in line with this axis, further to the west, is the church of St Benignus (now Benedict) (centre tower in **45**). The significance of this alignment will be considered in later pages, when the various stages of the development of the Abbey precinct are examined. The medieval churches still survive in part as ruins; they can be studied at leisure. They have been thoroughly discussed elsewhere from an architectural point of view, and there is an excellent detailed model showing their original appearance in the Abbey Museum (**colour plate 29**). Nothing, however, can be seen of the earlier churches and other features of Anglo-Saxon times and so they are discussed more fully here.

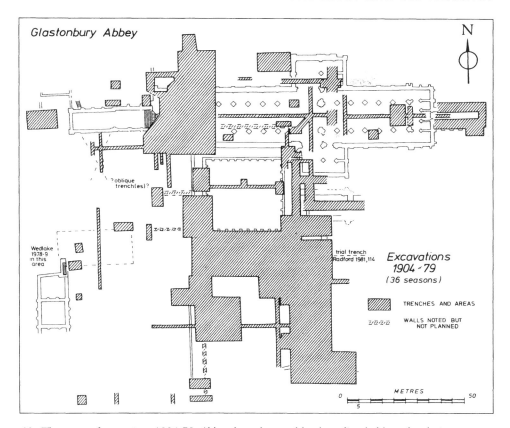

41 *The extent of excavations 1904-79. Although much ground has been disturbed by archaeologists, excavations did not in most places go as deep as the natural subsoil and there is still much undisturbed ground in other parts of the precinct.* After Aston and Leech, 1977

The Anglo-Saxon churches

It was known from medieval written sources (p.37) that there were churches earlier than the one whose ruins survive; and there were some clues as to where such structures might be found. It was realised at an early stage that there was no chance of finding the 'old church', the *vetusta ecclesia*. This would, in its predicted location, have been destroyed by the crypt of the Lady Chapel of medieval date. But floors and walls were found to the east of its supposed site which were soon identified as Anglo-Saxon.

In view of the extensive and massive disturbance of the ground in Norman and later times it was remarkable that anything was left at all. But to the great satisfaction of the excavators a good deal did survive, at a depth of over 2m (6.5ft). The reason for this was that the thirteenth-century builders had raised the level of the nave area by the deposition of thousands of tons of clay derived from their deep foundation trenches.

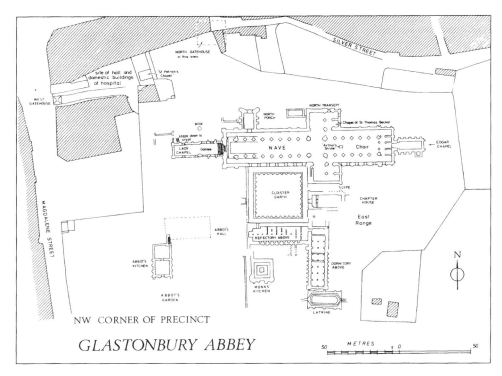

42 *Plan of the Abbey ruins as laid out today in relation to other features in the north-west corner of the precinct.* After Aston and Leech, 1977

The Anglo-Saxon remains were found in the spaces between the much larger foundation trenches of the later churches. These structures are very important to the understanding of pre-Conquest Glastonbury, and indeed of the Early Christian church in Britain.

Earlier Anglo-Saxon churches

We begin with a structure which has been totally destroyed: the *vetusta ecclesia* (Latin), or *ealdechurche* (Old English). The 'Old Church' thus named is referred to by medieval writers (p.61). It appears to have been held in great veneration; Henry de Blois for example made a grant to the Abbey 'to pay for a candle to burn night and day before the image of the Blessed Virgin Mary in the Old Church at Glastonbury'. It survived until the fire of 1184 and was thus still visible to visitors before this date, notably to William of Malmesbury, in the earlier part of the twelfth century.

Its original date is unknown. Many writers have accepted the traditional view that this building was the nucleus of a British monastery that preceded the Anglo-Saxon institution of the late seventh to eighth centuries AD. They would thus date it to the earlier seventh century or even before; the most optimistic would take it back to the first century, to the days of Joseph of Arimathea.

There is no evidence that it was, in fact, earlier than the seventh century. It was suggested above (p.78) that the Abbey site represents a development secondary to that on the Tor, which flourished in the sixth century. William of Malmesbury describes Ina's church (of the early eighth century) as secondary to it; this could still allow it to be associated with a British rather than an Anglo-Saxon administration.

Earlier accounts describe the church as of wattle construction, that is of intertwined wooden rods as used in the construction of hurdles, probably sealed with clay (daub), and roofed with organic material such as thatch, shingles or turf. Such buildings are well known in the archaeological record, from prehistoric to medieval (and even later) times. Such a building is unlikely to have survived intact for some five centuries. One account indeed describes it as having been encased in lead, a treatment that was also said to have been provided for the earliest church at York. One of the twelfth-century *Lives* of Dunstan describes it, however, as a wooden church, a detail repeated by William of Malmesbury. This would perhaps imply a more substantial (possibly rebuilt) construction, more like a Scandinavian stave church, of timber planks laid vertically or horizontally. Traces of such buildings, represented by post-holes or timber emplacements, have often been found beneath their successors in stone.

The location and size of the *vetusta ecclesia* in all published sources is as shown in the plans (see **43**). This position is based firstly on the medieval references. These describe the Lady Chapel as having been built around or on the site of the destroyed earlier building, To encase an earlier famous building or its site is a well-known procedure; and the magnificent late twelfth-century Lady Chapel (**colour plate 11**) is indeed a splendid successor to the older church.

The second source of information for the location of the Old Church is the text engraved on the brass plate, recorded by earlier writers but now lost (p.43). It consisted of two pieces of brass, an octagonal upper part and a separate base (see **20**). It was originally fixed in place by eleven projecting pierced bosses set around the edge.

The shape is peculiar and was presumably symbolic. It seems to reflect either an anthropomorphic form, such as a head and shoulder image; or more probably a cross set on a stepped base. It is suggested that the plate may have been protected by a movable cover, on which the symbolism of bust or cross could have been made more explicit by, for example, a painting. The inscription (p.43-44) indicates that the purpose of the plate (apart from providing an outline of the Abbey's early history) was to indicate where it was believed that the east end of the *vetusta ecclesia* had been as well as its dimensions (60ft by 26ft, 18 by 8m), and the distance of the mid-point of the church to the plate (48ft, 15m). The inscription further implies that the plate was fixed to a pillar or column. The existence of such a pillar is supported by a discovery made in 1921 of a circular column-base, in an appropriate position on the north side.

There is, however, some ambiguity in the inscription as to where the pillar was, and some scholars believe it was on the south side; both locations are accordingly

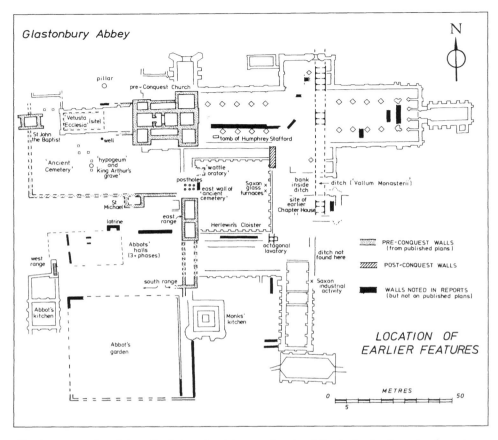

43 *A summary plan of the earlier features found in excavation, in relation to the standing ruins shown in* **42**; *this is Roger Leech's attempt to locate the positions of walls discovered, using many inadequate excavation reports.* After Aston and Leech, 1977 and Radford, 1981

shown on one of the plans (**44**). The interest of the inscription and its location is that it is the first 'tourist guide' to the Abbey placed at the original east end of the Lady Chapel. Pilgrims could stand at this spot and 'gaze with reverential awe on this most sacred spot, and to recall the amazing story of the past'.

These sources date, however, from times long after the Old Church had been destroyed. The only eye-witness, William of Malmesbury, in fact describes 'Ina's church' as appended to the older building; implying that the *vetusta ecclesia* lay directly west of the stone building shortly to be discussed.

Its precise size is, of course, unknown; the outline shown (see **50**), of some 18 by 8m (60 by 26ft), is that of the interior of the present Lady Chapel (approximately the size indicated on the brass plate). This would be rather large for a 'wattle' building, but not out of place for a substantial wooden one.

The appearance of the Old Church can only be guessed at, but this has not prevented speculation. Earlier 'visions' by Spelman (**46** & **47**) are interesting not so

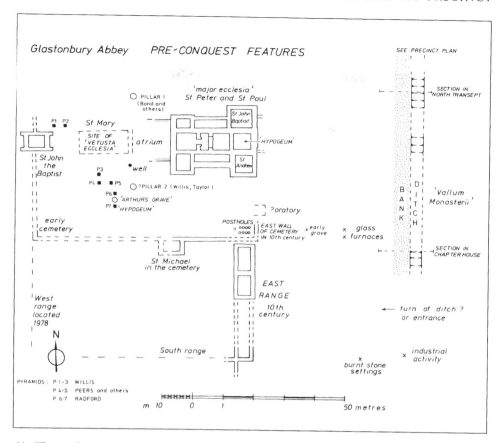

44 *The pre-Conquest layouts here shown in isolation, with the alternative locations of the pyramids and pillar as conjectured by various scholars.* After Leech and others

much for what they tell us about the appearance of the church, as the light they shed on later perceptions. A new version is shown in **48**. The only early 'pictorial' representation is that provided by the Glastonbury seal (see below).

Another detail that may be added – and a remarkable one – is that William of Malmesbury tells us that the church had a 'pavement of polished stone, in which were stones interlaid with triangles and squares, and set with lead'. Inside the church were also various memorials of saints and other distinguished persons (see p.114). The gifts of various post-Conquest abbots, and especially of Henry de Blois, ensured that the interior was richly decorated with religious ornaments and hangings.

The crypt of the twelfth-century Lady Chapel (see **59**), probably destroyed all the area of the *vetusta ecclesia*. Had this not been so, (in the sixteenth century, see p.105) it would have been possible for archaeology to have determined much about the character of the *vetusta ecclesia*. Finally, the position of the well (p.106 and **44**) in relation to the area of the Old Church should be noted.

45 *The ruins from the east; note the tower of St Benignus' Church in the centre*

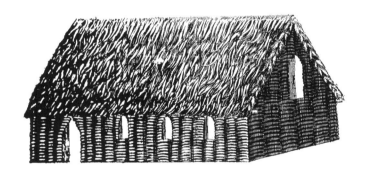

46 *The Old Church, or* vetusta ecclesia, *with wattle walls and reed thatch, as envisaged by Henry Spelman in the mid-seventeenth century*

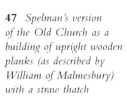

47 *Spelman's version of the Old Church as a building of upright wooden planks (as described by William of Malmesbury) with a straw thatch*

Sources later than William (including the brass plate inscription) embellished the history of the church by references to a church built by St David (possibly fourth century), added as a chancel to the *vetusta ecclesia*, and one to the 'twelve hermits' (p.61). It is unlikely that these ever existed.

The former is located in these later sources as somewhere between the *vetusta ecclesia* and Ina's church. The latter, dedicated to Sts Peter and Paul, was also east of the Old Church.

The Glastonbury seal

In the Gloucester Record Office is a Charter of Robert of Winchester, abbot 1171–8. Attached to it is a seal; a new photograph by the Record Office is reproduced here (**49**). At face value, it is the earliest known representation of the Abbey before the fire of 1184. While such depictions are usually formal, symbolic, schematic and derivative, they can provide hints, if not of what the Abbey actually looked like, at least of what was credible to contemporaries. At best, it may have elements of actual representation.

48 *The 'pyramids', with part of the cemetery and an appropriate procession, as they would have been seen in the eighth to ninth century. The Old Church is seen in the background, with a well outside its south-east corner. The church survived until the fire of 1184; the pyramids were by then in a weathered state.*
Judith Dobie

49 *Seal of Glastonbury Abbey (late twelfth century); it apparently shows the west end of the church at this time (before the fire of 1184)*

The seal appears to show an elevation of one or more buildings. It has been suggested that what is represented is the elevation of the west end of the church as it was in the 1170s or before. On the left is the wooden lead-covered *vetusta ecclesia*. The central part of this shows two windowed turrets with 'pepper-box' caps. There is a doorway between them, with a window above. On the extreme left is what may be a northern porticus (see **52**); and above the whole what may be the lower part of a large gable end, or perhaps an upper storey, with a further doorway or window in the centre – or is this another capped turret?

To the right (i.e. to the south of the church) is a tower with a western doorway, a first-floor window, and a double-windowed third storey, capped by a pyramidal tower. This has been suggested to be the bell-tower of Henri de Blois, abbot from 1126 to 1171 (p.45); this is recorded as having stood in the ancient cemetery. To the right of this again, further south, are one or two vertical lines which, it has been suggested, represent one or both of the famous 'pyramids'.

If these interpretations of the picture on the seal are correct, it is clear that the Lady Chapel, built after the fire, echoed elements of the *vetusta ecclesia* as it existed in its latter days, notably the turrets (see **colour plate 11**).

Even if the seal is not accepted as a true representation, it is at least the earliest 'picture' of the Abbey, antedating post-Dissolution views by several hundred years.

Later Anglo-Saxon churches

The foundations of various dates are separated on the basis of variations in mortar and on certain structural relationships (**50**, **51** & **52**). The surviving fragments of foundation are separated one from another by large areas of destruction brought about by the digging of the foundations of the Norman and later medieval churches.

1 *Glastonbury Tor: aerial view.* Mick Aston

2 *Flooding to the west of Glastonbury; photograph taken from the Tor in August 1968. Wirral Hill is in the distance*

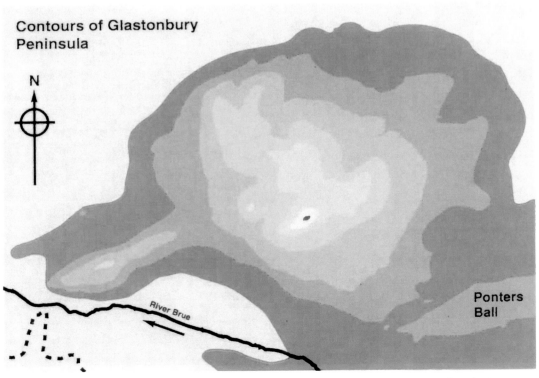

Contours of Glastonbury Peninsula

N

River Brue

Ponters Ball

3 *Contour plan of Glastonbury peninsula; note the narrow channel of the River Brue separating this from the Street area to the south-west, and the broad link to the 'mainland' to the south-east*

4 *A reconstruction drawing of Glastonbury Lake Village showing log boats arriving laden with swans.*
Drawn by A. Forester, 1911

5 *British postage stamp showing the Holy Thorn*

6 *The dark age settlement on the Tor (sixth century AD). In the foreground is the spring of Chalice Well, as it was before the medieval well-house was built over it. Supplies are being transported to the Tor summit by packhorse, including water from the spring.* Judith Dobie

7 *Glastonbury Tor: the Anglo-Saxon monastery from the east; on the summit in the foreground is a wheel-headed cross. Below, on the summit's shoulder, are the monastic buildings; the largest is a church or communal building, with several smaller cells and other structures.* Judith Dobie

8 *Glastonbury Tor: St Michael's Church and associated buildings, from the south-west.* Judith Dobie

9 *Glastonbury Tor viewed from Sharpham.* Painted by W. Wheatley *c.*1840.
Somerset Archaeology and Natural History Service

10 *The Abbey ruins from the east; the central tower is that of the church of St Benignus*

11 *The Lady Chapel from the south. This was built after the fire of 1184, and consecrated in 1186. It is one of the finest buildings known in Transitional Romanesque style*

12   *St Mary Magdalene Hospital; the original medieval cubicles were converted into the row of joined cottages seen here*

13 *The exhumation of 'Arthur' in 1191. The skeletons of 'Arthur and Guinevere' have been found in a wooden coffin. A monk is pulling out Guinevere's yellow hair; another is showing the lead cross to the assembled monks. In the background, work is still taking place on the Lady Chapel, built after the fire of 1184, and consecrated in 1186.* Judie Dobie

14 *Beckery: the grave excavated in 1967 which provided the nucleus of the timber and stone chapels; it may have been that of the founder of the monastery in the eighth or nineth century*

15 *The foundations of the excavated chapels at Beckery from the north-west. The outer rectangular chapel was built around a two-cell chapel of late Anglo-Saxon period; inside the latter are the post-holes and timber slots of the earliest wooden chapel or tomb-shrine, inside which was the grave shown above (**14**)*

16 *A finely carved Purbeck marble panel depicting Romanesque-style arches. Found at Glastonbury Abbey*

17 *A carved stone effigy of 'Jack Stagg' which once adorned the top of an earlier market cross at the bottom of Glastonbury High Street. Jack Stagg is though to represent Bacchus – the Roman god of wine*

18 *A finely carved head depicting a medieval monk from Glastonbury Abbey*

19 *Carved stone head probably depicting a saint. Found at Glastonbury Abbey*

20 *Lead Bulla of Pope Calistus III (1445-1458)*

21 *Lead Bulla of Pope Calistus III depicting Sts Paul and Peter*

22 *An eight-legged starfish made of lead found at Glastonbury Abbey. It probably represents a symbol of pilgrimmage*

23 *Medieval glazed floor tile from Glastonbury Abbey depicting three lions rampant denoting royal connections*

24 *Medieval glazed floor tile from Glastonbury Abbey depicting an elephant with a castellated platform on its back*

25 *Meare Fish House (fourteenth century). This was near to Meare Pool and other waterways. It was used by the abbey as a base for fishing activities, and for the salting and storage of fish.*

26 *Obscured view of the Abbot's Kitchen, the only one of the abbey buildings to survive the Dissolution*

27 *The medieval Tithe barn was one of the most important buildings in the management of the monastic estate. The barn was the focus for dealing with the harvest and ensuring that one tenth – the tithe – was paid to the abbey. Glastonbury was one of the wealthiest estates in medieval England. This barn is one of the finest examples of medieval barns in the country and the existing roof is dated to 1361 by dendrochronology*

28 *A view of the western elevation of Glastonbury Abbey Barn. This barn now forms part of the Somerset Rural Life Museum.* Somerset County Museums Service

29 *Model of Glastonbury Abbey as it may have looked in the fifteenth century. This model is on display in the Glastonbury Abbey Visitor Centre.* Somerset County Museums Service and Glastonbury Abbey Trustees

The problem facing any student of Glastonbury is how to join up the pieces, and how to interpret the restored results.

The first reliable reference to the building or rebuilding of a church at Glastonbury is to the work of King Ina of Wessex. It was in his reign (688–726) that Somerset came under full Anglo-Saxon political and military domination; he had political reasons for taking an interest in Glastonbury. The walls shown in black (**50**) are possibly to be identified with his work; the floor of the main part, shown stippled, was rendered on its surface with a thin reddish facing of lime mortar containing pounded brick. This is reminiscent of the reddish brick-tempered mortar (*opus signinum*) familiar in Roman structures everywhere in Europe; the use of such a 'Roman' technique reflects the Italian and Gaulish background of the work of this period in Britain.

This characteristic red floor material and the proportions of this church are similar to those of the early churches in Kent, built in the seventh to eighth centuries, following Augustine's conversion of the court of King Aethelbert at Canterbury.

The church (**50**), as thus defined, consists of a nave (G) with a step (H) leading up into a presbytery (J). The two outlying wall fragments to north and south (E and E′) are plausibly interpreted as the outer walls of porticus. These are side-chapels, used to provide altars, or for burials, and are a characteristic feature of many Anglo-Saxon churches. The western limits of this building are unknown; as

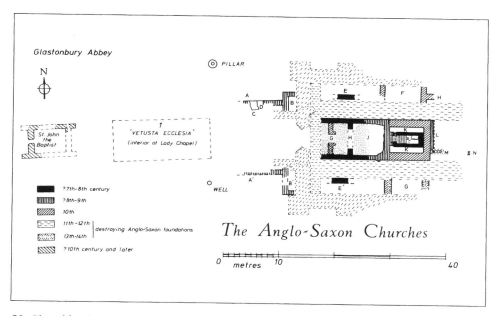

50 *Plan of foundations of the Anglo-Saxon churches, as known from excavation. Only St John the Baptist was not partly destroyed by later medieval building. The site of the* vetusta ecclesia *was totally removed by the sixteenth-century crypt of the Lady Chapel; and the later church added to it on its east side was badly disturbed by Norman and later church building. The different phases were shown by variations in mortar or construction. After Peers, Clapham and Radford*

51 *The main part of the Anglo-Saxon church as excavated in the 1920s; it will be seen how deep the remains were beneath the present ground surface*

also is the original form of the east end, whether an apse (as in **55**), or a rectilinear sanctuary. The *hypogeum* (X) is discussed separately below (p.101).

Later work used a distinctive mauve mortar. An atrium (a square courtyard) was added at the west end (A, A'); there appears to have been an entrance to this on the north side (C, D). Two more porticus were added (B, B'), of wider north–south dimension than the earlier ones. The east end was joined to the *hypogeum* (X).

In the nave, an L-shaped foundation wall (**52**) may have been for a screen or some other partition, marking the west end of the monks' choir of Dunstan's church, with one or more steps rising from the nave to the choir.

Another change of mortar signifies further alterations and additions at the east end. The *hypogeum* was now filled in and paved over (see below) and a wide and deep foundation made around this area for the tower recorded as having been built by Dunstan during his abbacy of 940-57. To the north and south were added two further porticus (F, G) with altars to St John the Baptist and St Andrew, and some extensions to the east (H, M, N). It is recorded that Dunstan built these porticus to make the width of the church 'square with its length'.

Only a few fragments of walling extend further east. Radford based his recon-structed plan (see **55**) on that of the French monastery of Cluny, of broadly contemporary date. The development of the Anglo-Saxon churches, between the seventh and tenth centuries, is shown in **52** in three stages.

Little is known of the superstructure of any of the Anglo-Saxon churches; they may have been wholly of stone, or partly of timber construction. The roofs were

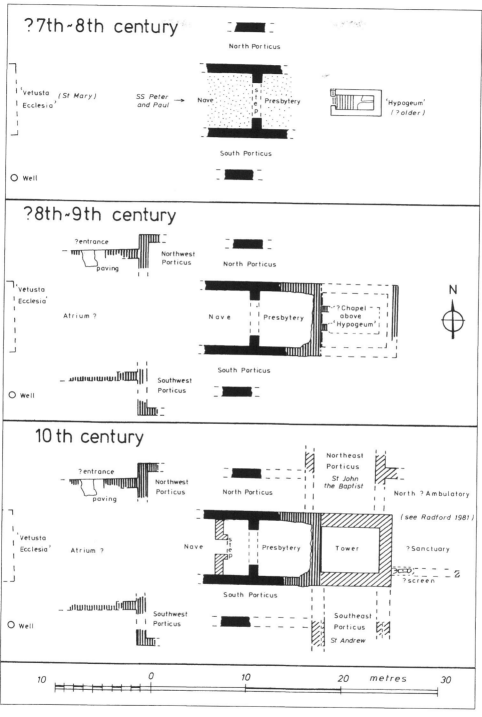

52 The *development of the Anglo-Saxon churches between the seventh and the tenth centuries AD; the east end of the* vetusta ecclesia *(the Old Church) is shown to the left. Dating is problematic, but the final phase should be the work of Abbot Dunstan.* PAR, 1991

presumably organic (turf, thatch, shingles) as no roof slates were found. The only evidence of interior decoration came from a thick layer of fallen wall plaster. This was painted in places with more than one layer; one piece displayed fragments of a draped figure.

St John the Baptist

This chapel (**53**) was built by Dunstan; it was to the west of the churches described above. It is orientated not with the other churches, but with the variant alignment of the *vetusta ecclesia* (see **50**). It is described by Dunstan's biographer (p.38) as being on the west side of the old church, 'with four equal angles to serve as a little beacon'. This description could apply to the plan as we now see it, with its rather odd east and west projections. Dunstan's version of this church may have been destroyed in the fire of 1184, the excavated version being its medieval replacement.

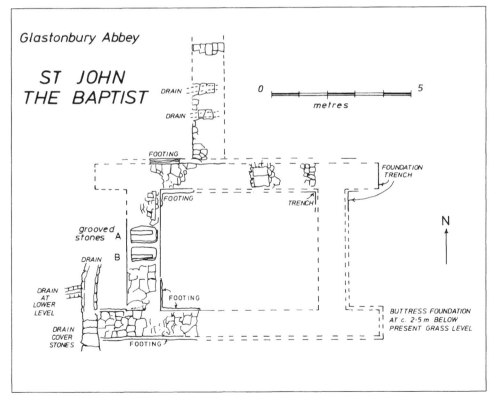

53 *The church of St John the Baptist at the west end of the ruins; it was possibly incorporated in a western gatehouse. The plan shows how carefully Bligh Bond recorded every stone, in advance of most archaeologists of his time. After Bligh Bond, 1913*

The plan is included for two reasons. Firstly, it is the actual evidence for an important building in the sequence; very little remained of the structure apart from footings and foundation trenches cut in the clay. Secondly, it illustrates the detailed recording made by Bligh Bond in the early part of the century – considerably in advance of any later excavator of Glastonbury.

Set into the west wall at sill level were two stones with grooves *c.*10cm (4in) deep (at A and B in **53**). These may have been used to key in the lower side slabs of an open arch, wide enough to allow foot passage. All this suggests that the chapel was originally the westerly point of entry into the monastic complex, giving access firstly to the raised cemetery area of Dunstan's layout and subsequently to the string of churches to the east. This would imply that it was really a gatehouse with a throughway, and a chapel above, in an upper storey.

The *hypogeum* or burial crypt

This small stone structure (**54**) was found, filled with rubble, beneath the tower of the late tenth century. It consists of a rectangular compartment, *c.*4 by 1.5m (13 by 5ft) internally, at least partly below the ground level (similar to some mausolea); there was an entrance at the west end. Here, set squarely within the doorway, and extending both into the interior and western exterior, was a massive stone coffin. This is later, however; its contents are discussed below in relation to mortuary practice (p.72).

The rectangular structure has been interpreted as a 'raised chapel with a shrine above a crypt entered by a narrow stair in the centre of the rising flight'. It has also been compared with the famous seventh- to eighth-century *hypogeum* at Poitiers in south-west France (**54**). This was erected by one Abbot Mellebaud as a mausoleum for himself, and contained the relics of 72 martyrs of the early church in that area. There is also at the east ends of both structures a slab on the outer side of the wall. At Poitiers this was seen as part of an arrangement by which the martyrs' tombs could be viewed through the head of a window at the east end; and a similar function is envisaged for the comparable slab at Glastonbury. The two ragged gaps in the north and south walls are also similar to recesses at Poitiers, for the setting of stone coffins.

The medieval churches

The evidence for a gradual expansion of the churches in pre-Conquest times has been discussed above (p.90-7). With the accession of the Norman abbots rebuilding was started from the east end, begun by Abbot Turstin around 1100 (**55**). He was remarkable for his disastrous relationship with the monks, culminating in the shooting down of several of them by his soldiers (p.46). The latter

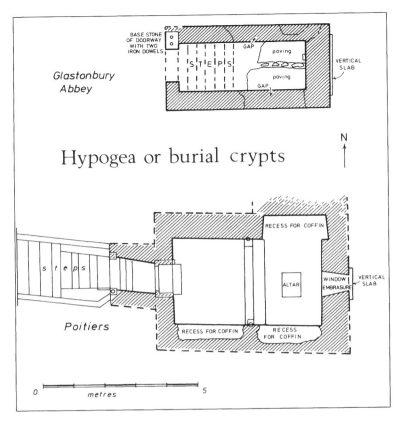

54 *The hypogeum or burial crypt at Glastonbury, compared with the well-known example at Poitiers. After Clapham*

seem to have been firing down from some sort of gallery, probably an upper level at the east end of Dunstan's church. Turstin's church was abandoned and demolished by Abbot Herlewin (*c.*1140); his great new Romanesque church (see **55**) now extended westwards, destroying much of the pre-Conquest complex.

Most of the Abbey of this time was destroyed in the great fire of 1184 (p.46). The new campaigns, begun at the end of the twelfth century, culminated in the buildings whose ruins can now be inspected (**55** and **colour plate 10**). The earliest of these post-fire buildings was the Lady Chapel.

The Lady Chapel (42)

Popularly called St Joseph's Chapel, this is a building of very high quality (**colour plate 11**) with fine decorative features. Its history and function will be summarised, and in particular, the remarkable crypt which lies below it, with a well to the south at the lower level.

The Lady Chapel was begun directly after the fire of 1184, and consecrated in 1186. This building, as already noted, destroyed the *vetusta ecclesia* in whatever form

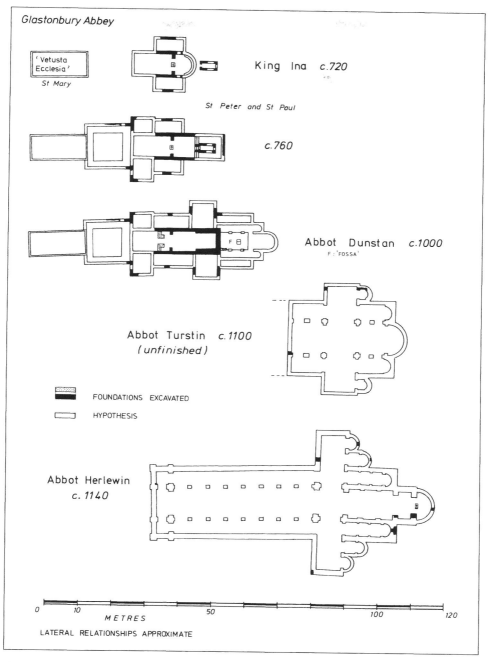

55 *The sequence of Anglo-Saxon and Norman churches, as interpreted and reconstructed by Ralegh Radford; the parts shaded black are all that was actually found; the rest of the plans are restored by analogy with other churches.* After Radford, 1981 and pers. comm., 1991

it survived in 1184. It was apparently erected directly over the site of the earlier building, perpetuating both its site and its dimensions.

Not surprisingly, the fame of the Old Church was such that the Lady Chapel was the first construction to be undertaken after the fire; and no expense was spared therefore to make it one of the finest buildings of its day in the transitional Romanesque style, a worthy successor to the Old Church, and appropriately given the same prestigious dedication to St Mary. It was originally quite separate from the main church to the east, without a chancel. But subsequently, in the thirteenth century, the two were linked by the structure known as the Galilee; the east part of this enclosed a great flight of steps leading up to the raised level of the nave. The Lady Chapel had two grand doorways, one opening south into the monks' cemetery, the other to the north, to the lay cemetery; and beyond to the north gate of the Abbey, and the High Street.

Adjoining the Chapel to the south, at its east end (**50**), was a well (see below). It will be argued that this may have already existed when the chapel was built. The foundations of the chapel extend to a depth of over 3m (10ft), in order to build on bedrock, rather than clay; but there is no evidence that there was originally a crypt.

In the interior of the Lady Chapel today (**57**) one looks down into the crypt, the floor level of the Lady Chapel having been totally removed (**58**). The work that can be seen now is that constructed by Abbot Bere around 1500. This extended not only under the four bays of the Lady Chapel but also under the two western bays of the Galilee. The vaults were roughly constructed; they raised

56 *The ruins of the north transept, from the north-west*

57 *The interior of the Lady Chapel from the east, with the crypt below; the floor which separated these has been entirely removed*

the floor of the Lady Chapel by *c.*50cm (20in), the height of the stone benches which extended around the interior. The vault sides were also made to slope up so that five windows could be inserted into the earlier work to light the crypt. An entrance to the north side was made, at the west end, down steps into the crypt. Access was also made from the crypt to the well.

In the period of destruction that followed the Dissolution, the crypt was wrecked and the vault and upper floors largely destroyed. When described in 1724 by William Stukeley it was full of water (probably from a spring – see below). He was told that many lead coffins had been brought up from the crypt. In 1825 the crypt was cleared (**59**) and the steps down to it from the north were widened. More burials were found in this operation (p.72) together with the well, now discussed in some detail.

St Joseph's Well (61)

In the work of 1825, a flight of underground steps was reported close to the southeast corner of the Lady Chapel, and the arch of a passage leading in the same direction from the crypt. A pit 3.65m (12ft) square was sunk to a depth of over 1.5m (5ft), which revealed the crown of a semicircular arch. Further exploration

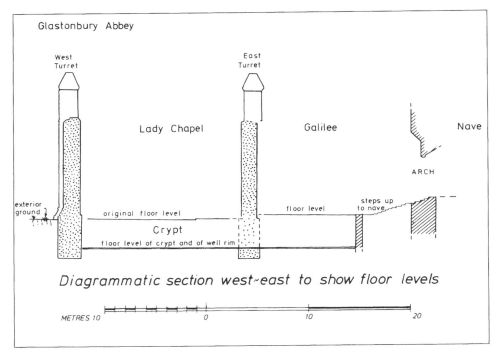

58 *Section through the Lady Chapel, Galilee and west end of the nave. This shows the depth of the Norman foundation, and the space excavated for the crypt c.1500.* After Willis, 1866

59 *The crypt under the Lady Chapel, as cleared in the early nineteenth century*

revealed the well below this, and the passage leading to it from the crypt was cleared of rubble. Not surprisingly the well was at once dubbed as 'holy', and attracted much public attention at the time, though the Roman Catholic clergy of the day were oddly at pains to assign it a more mundane function such as for officiating monks to wash vestments.

The well was said to be *c*.1.5m (5ft) deep; this may, however, have been the depth of the water, rather than the well itself – a point of some importance, as will be seen below. It is approached now from the crypt through a passage over 5m (16ft) long, where there is evidence of considerable rebuilding in modern times. The well is seen on the left (east), as a circular basin, 71cm (28in) in diameter; the rim is flush with a surrounding platform in a recess – this is over 3m (10ft) below the present ground level. The shaft is not set centrally in the platform, but lies on its south side; that is with more space to its north (**60**).

The well is fed by a spring issuing from a hole in the natural rock. There was an overflow conduit at the top which led to a 'great drain' surrounding the Abbey. Perhaps it was the neglect of these arrangements which caused the crypt to flood.

Over the recess is the arch found in 1825 (**61**). This is of the same style and size as the Norman windows of the chapel above, with elaborate chevron decoration. It was not, however, put over the recess in Norman times. It is likely that it was in fact the east window of the Lady Chapel, taken down when this was extended to the east as the Galilee, in the thirteenth century. On the outside of the Lady Chapel there are cuts in the Norman masonry, showing where there has been a structure attached to the chapel; it is suggested that this was the entrance porch to a well-house below ground, reached by the steps reported in 1825.

From the passage the well area is left by way of a newel stair up to the west; then along a higher passage to an interesting flight of steep steps (1–11 in **60**). These lead to a doorway to the north, which would originally have given on to the chapel floor; from the steps is a slab which provides access to the south exterior; the ground-floor access here would also have led to the Chapel floor. All this work appears to be of late medieval date.

The point of this discussion is to suggest that the well may be an early feature; either contemporary with, or dating from before, the fire of 1184; it may even be much earlier, that is Roman. This would put the well into a very different category. The association of a spring with religious activity is attested from prehistoric times, through Roman temples, to the use of wells and springs as focal points in churches and cathedrals. We need look no further than Wells for an example.

If the well is pre-Norman, it would have lain outside the south-east corner of the *vetusta ecclesia*, (**50**) and may in fact (if Roman) have determined its location. If the ground level of the Old Church was, as seems likely, only a little below that of the ground floor of the Lady Chapel, the well as seen today would then have been more than 3m (10ft) below and must have been approached by steps; though it may have been originally built up so that its head was at that time higher.

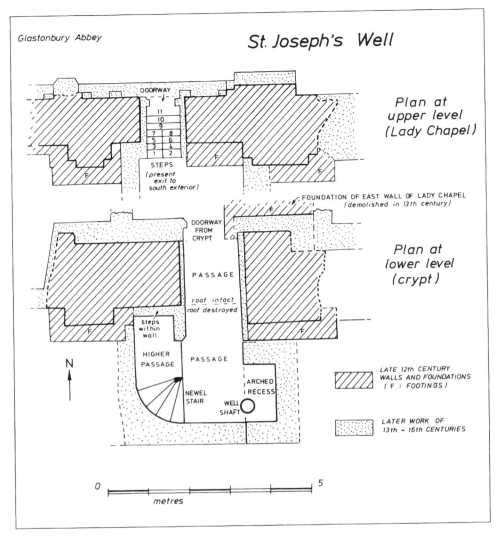

60 *St Joseph's Well, in the crypt of the Lady Chapel; there is access to this from the crypt, from the Chapel above, and from the cemetery area to the south.* After Willis, 1866

In September 1991 and June 1992, in an attempt to resolve some of these problems, the well was examined to determine the nature of its structure. The rim, or well-head, now has a thick coating of calcite accretion but removal of part of this showed that it was of segmented stones, of oolitic limestone. Below this, at water level, the stonework of the well has been partly dissolved away by the movement of the water. The water (*c.*60cm (24in) deep) was baled out and at the base was mud and rubble with hundreds of coins of 1960 and later. This layer was removed down to a depth of *c.*1.50m (5ft) or more and it was seen that the shaft of the well (65–66cm (25–26in) in diameter) was lined with skilfully laid pieces of Lias limestone. The overall appearance was very similar to that of Roman wells

61 *The arched recess over the well, in the early nineteenth century*

excavated in the area. If the well existed as early as this, however, it is likely to have had its well-head at or near ground level. In this case it must have been truncated (perhaps when the chapel foundations were dug) and its head reset at its present level.

To conclude, these new observations support the idea that the well is of early (pre-Norman) date; it may well be a primary feature of the abbey site, perhaps even pre-dating the *vetusta ecclesia*.

Other early features

It must be remembered that the churches were, like those of the many later abbeys of medieval date, part of an extensive institutional complex – the monastery. The plan of this after the fire of 1184 is now reasonably complete (see **42**), but that of the pre-Conquest monastery much less so. Traces of earlier buildings and features have, however, been found. The most important is the claustral layout, which is discussed further below (p.115).

The cemetery

The cloister is separated from the church by the area of the ancient cemetery (**43**). The graves of important personages would have been either in the churches or in the cemetery on the south side of the church; there was also a cemetery to the north of the church, notionally for lay people.

The original extent of the cemetery (in the seventh to eighth centuries) is unknown. Numerous graves have been found in the main area south of the

Anglo-Saxon church, and one is recorded well to the east (west of the glass furnaces in **44**). In the tenth century, however, the cemetery was enclosed by a wall and a gatehouse chapel was set in the western side, at the end of the line of churches (St John the Baptist, p.97).

The southern cemetery was at this time defined as an area *c.*70 by 20m (230 by 66ft), and much of it was raised more than a metre. This was done by Dunstan explicitly to seal the early graves of the 'saints'. The result was to create a raised platform revetted by a wall on the south side; the northern edge sloped downwards to the older ground level (this is reflected in the present-day level of the grass). The new arrangement has been interpreted as a planned refocusing of the pilgrimage centre of the monastery, perhaps with paths set over the raised area.

Incorporated into the south (revetment) wall, on the south side and extending into the cloister, (see below) was the Chapel of St Michael in the cemetery (**43** & **44**). While this may also have had an early origin, the remains found were all of thirteenth- and fourteenth-century date; there had been a vault here filled with charnel of around 50 individuals.

The cemetery, while its primary function was that of burial, served also (as today) as a place of visitation and as a memorial to the venerated dead. In later pages the character of the graves and memorials, both in the ancient cemetery and in later contexts, will be described.

Independently of features related to burial or commemoration, there were also oratories, or minor chapels, in the cemetery area; four were noted in the excavations, but there is some overlap between these and the tomb-shrines associated with burial. The best-preserved example on the plan (**44**) was *c.*5.2 by 4m (17 by 13ft), built around a frame of wooden uprights 1.2m (4ft) apart, with a roughly trodden floor.

Mortuary practice in the Abbey

The general term mortuary practice is used to cover all the ways in which successive generations disposed of the dead, with more or less ceremony. Since a wholly Christian context of the seventh century and later is under discussion, we may assume that burial was by inhumation, with bodies extended on their backs (but see Beckery, p.148), arms in various positions and orientated with heads to the west. The evidence from Glastonbury, though slight, is an important (and early) contribution to the now rapidly increasing body of data for Christian burial in Britain and elsewhere.

The earliest graves found in the ancient cemetery were numerous. They were dug into the old ground surface below the earth of Dunstan's heightening of the area. They were roughly lined with slabs of Lias limestone set on edge and covered at the level of the old ground surface with further slabs (sometimes one slab served two graves). A further group of such rough 'cist' graves was found dug from the higher level of the cemetery, and should be of the tenth century or later. Such stone-lined and capped graves – the stone slabs forming the equivalent of rough coffins – are a common feature of early Christian cemeteries from the late Roman period into medieval times, and hundreds have been found in early church sites, open cemeteries and monastic sites in the whole of Britain. There were also at least two graves of what were believed to be more important people in rectangular post-built mausolea, which would have been visible above the ground. One of these was equated with the supposed grave of 'Arthur' found in 1191 (p.55). Many medieval graves were found in the excavations, in wooden or stone coffins (or in 'pseudo'-coffins made of blocks of stone), some with recesses for the head.

An especially interesting group was found in 1825. Steps which led down to the crypt of the Lady Chapel were being repaired, and lengthened into a passage extending to the north (as seen today). Eighteen coffins were found, one 2.5m (8ft) long internally; they were made of oak 7.5cm (3in) thick, preserved in the damp ground. Under the head and shoulders of each skeleton was a bundle of wood shavings, perhaps the stuffing of pillows. Beneath and to the right side of each skeleton was also a rod of thorn or hazel, of the same length as the coffin. Such rods or wands have been found in several sites in Britain and Scandinavia with medieval ecclesiastics, but their function or symbolism is unknown.

Another grave dated to the twelfth century contained a skeleton with buckles which had held up stockings. This was believed to be the grave of Abbot Seffrid (d.1150). Another, possibly that of Abbot Vigor (d.1223), was found in the chapter house with a staff of base metal.

A very large coffin, as already noted, was found inserted into the rectangular *hypogeum* structure under Dunstan's tower (p.100). This was *c*.2 by 0.7m (over 6 by 2ft) externally; the east end was rounded, and the west end had a head recess. Inside were parts of 17 skeletons; the skulls were at the west end, larger bones at both ends and smaller bones in the middle. The individuals represented were all tall sturdy adult males aged up to 60 years old. Such a charnel deposit is frequently found when graves have been disturbed in building operations. The identity of the original occupant of this great coffin is unknown.

One of the later graves in the church was on the south side of the nave – a large walled grave *c*.1.5m (5ft) deep. At the base was a wooden coffin with elaborate metal bindings and the heavy, possibly mutilated bones of an adult male; this grave would have had an elaborate cover slab. It is believed to be the grave of Humphrey Stafford, one of the Monmouth rebels, who was beheaded at Gloucester in 1469.

Apart from the report on the bones of 17 males in the stone coffin found in 1928 by Sir Arthur Fawcett, none of the others has been expertly examined; nor are there details of other aspects of grave ritual (such as arm position) which would be recorded nowadays.

Other early graves are known from written sources but cannot now be equated with any excavated burials. For instance, Sts 'Patrick' and 'Indracht' were buried in 'pyramids' (see below) on either side of the altar of the oldest church.

Abbot Tica, who died c.760, was 'buried in the right corner of the great church', 'near the entry to the old church'. The 17 sturdy male skeletons found in the stone coffin in the *hypogeum* (p.101) are likely originally to have been from similar high-status graves in the church. Most important of all were the graves of kings (p.63).

There are records of medieval excavation of graves. The Norman Abbot Aethelweard decided to excavate King Edgar's tomb. He found the body well preserved; and (as was customary) hacked it up to make it fit into a reliquary he had provided. In response to this violation, the body began to bleed profusely; Aethelweard became insane, and subsequently broke his neck in a fall.

Such 'translations' of important people were quite usual; several are recorded in the pages of Bede, the most famous of these being St Cuthbert. A Glastonbury example is the translation of the bones of St Benignus from Meare by Abbot Turstin in 1091, to the new church dedicated in his honour.

Apart from translation, the bones of 'holy' persons often became important relics, the focus of pilgrimage and also of rivalry between different houses. As noted above, Glastonbury and Canterbury both claimed to possess the bones of Dunstan himself, and this led to bitter arguments and accusations of theft and misrepresentation. What may have been a receptacle for such relics was found in the church (*fossa* on **55**).

Not surprisingly, as with 'Arthur', bones were dug for deliberately. The grave of Joseph of Arimathea, and the relics it would contain, was sought for on several occasions, for political as well as for religious reasons (p.59). The first attempt recorded was made by one J. Blome in June 1345; he obtained a royal licence to dig within the precinct, provided he did not endanger the church or buildings, and that the work was done with the consent of the Abbot and convent.

This attempt may have been initiated because of a prophecy manufactured in the fourteenth century ('Melkin's prophecy'): that Joseph's grave would be found in the southern cemetery in the same place as 'Arthur's', '*in linea bifurcata*'. This has been taken to mean (if puzzlingly) 'in or on a forked line'; but the Latin may be more plausibly interpreted as 'in an undergarment, close-fitting, made of linen and divided into two flaps below like a dalmatic'!

A document of c.1420 purports to be a response by Abbot Frome to a request for information about Joseph's grave from no less a person than Henry V. The King had heard that the monks had dug in the cemetery in 1419 and wanted to know more. The letter recapitulates the early legends concerning the Abbey. An interesting detail here concerns the 'wattle church': 'all those buried there . . . have with them twigs in their tombs, namely one according to the length of the body, the other in a cross direction under the feet . . . ;' this is reminiscent of the 'wands' found in 1825 (p.72).

The location of Joseph is as follows: 'next to the southern corner of the oratory with prepared wattle above the venerable Virgin . . .'. Frome goes on to describe the excavation of 1419; this is a passage rich in detail for the archaeologist, of what someone in the fifteenth century thought graves might contain, even if the account is a total invention:

> In the south side of the cemetery of the old church were discovered three ancient coffins in the earth at a depth of about 17 feet. The coffin which lay in the northern part contained the bones of a decayed and perished man, the bones arranged according to the manner of death. Near the bones of the head there was an abundance of grains of green and scented herbs with their seeds. In the coffin which lay in the middle there were contained the bones of twelve corpses, which were so ingeniously and so finely arranged within the casket that, after their extraction, in truth nobody there knew how to arrange them again in the aforesaid casket. In the third coffin which lay to the south were the bones of a decayed and perished individual lying in the manner of nature, and away from the middle of the aforesaid corpse towards the head a great abundance of fluid, which appeared as fresh blood to those present in that place both by its colour and substance. All these coffins were found outside the Chapel. Within the Chapel, however, under the southern corner of the altar, another coffin was found with the bones of a decayed man. This coffin was adorned most excellently beyond the others with linen cloth inside all over. And because it prevailed over all of them in delicacy of scent and eminence of place it was enclosed in another large coffin until clearer notice of it will be able to be had in the future.

Surprisingly, Frome did not directly claim that the last-named burial was that of Joseph; though there is mention in a later account of an identifying lead plaque similar to that of 'Arthur'. The desire to find Joseph lingers: a request to look for his grave was made to the Abbey Trustees in 1991, but was refused.

Even the earth from the cemetery was regarded as having power of salvation or healing. One Rainald of Marksbury, a Crusader, was captured by a Sultan; it was agreed that he could be released if he went back to Glastonbury and returned with a gloveful of soil from the cemetery.

The cemetery, which had been 'as important and a vital part of the monastic heritage at Glastonbury as the library' fell into neglect after the Dissolution. In 1777 the antiquary Revd J. Whitaker was shown the location of the burial ground on the north side of the church, then a kitchen garden to the White Hart. 'Thus', he commented, 'vegetables for visitors to the ruins were raised from soil impregnated with the bodies of monks, bishops, nobles and kings innumerable.'

In this century, the cemetery, on both north and south sides of the church, has been returned to a state more appropriate to its former fame, with well-mown turf. Some configuration of the raised cemetery of Dunstan (p.43) was restored after the excavations. The only grave now recorded in the turfed area is, alas, that of 'Arthur'.

Memorials and pyramids

Many of the graves would have been marked by memorials of stone or other material. None remains today, but those inside the church were recorded in the sixteenth century, together with the associated tombs. There are listed those of King Edmund and Edmund Ironside in the presbytery, flanking that of 'Arthur' and many abbots and other notable monks and lay persons.

The most famous memorials are those outside the church known as the 'pyramids'; equally notorious is their association with the supposed grave of Arthur, with the lead cross. The inscriptions on these have already been discussed in their historical context in chapter 4, and their association with Arthur in chapter 5. It remains now to consider their character and location. The first mention of them is by William of Malmesbury in the earlier twelfth century; by his day they were already of some antiquity; a date in the eighth or ninth century is suggested in chapter 4 (p.43).

There were two 'pyramids', he says, a few feet from the church, 'bordering the monks' cemetery'. The one nearer the church ('threatening ruin from its great age') was c.7.9m (26ft) high, with five stages; the one further away was c.5.5m (18ft) high, with four stages. It is clear that the meaning of pyramid in this context is that of a tapering stone shaft. In other contexts these are called high crosses, such as that at Bewcastle or those of Ireland. The stages were, according to William, decorated with sculpture and inscriptions (p.41).

It is not known if William measured the heights of the pyramids, and looked closely at the inscriptions (i.e. with a ladder provided by the monks); or whether he guessed the heights and made out what he could from the ground. But it may be assumed that they were substantial monuments between 5m and 8m high. His description implies that one was nearer to the church, and one was further away; they must therefore presumably have been either in an east-west alignment to the west, south-west or south of the church; or in a north-south alignment on the south side.

Later writers also describe the pyramids, together with rather ambiguous details of their location. William of Worcester (1480) (p.53) saw two stone 'crosses', 'hollowed', 'where the bones of Arthur were buried, and where Joseph of Arimathea lies buried'. He locates them 'opposite the second window on the south side in the churchyard'. He describes the Lady Chapel as having seven large windows on each side. On the south side, the westernmost four of these survive. By the second window he may mean the second from the west, looking from the south; or the second from the east, one that is no longer extant. The former would seem the more likely but it has a large doorway beneath it (see **colour plate 11**). It has been suggested that the pyramids are unlikely to have been directly opposite a major entrance. This favours a counting from the east; this would, however, place them well to the east of the *vetusta ecclesia*, and the doorway argument does not seem to carry any weight. Spelman (in the mid-seventeenth century) provided his own view of what they looked like (see **19**). A new reconstruction is now attempted (see **48**), but it must be regarded as hardly less fanciful.

Whitaker later (1777) tells of a visit to Glastonbury where his guide pointed out two cavities a few feet from the north-west angle of the church; from these spots, said the guide, two pyramids had recently been removed for use as gate posts or cottage props. He (the guide) had seen them himself before their removal; they were *c*.3m (9–10ft) high. So much for sightings; we now turn to what a series of scholars have made of these descriptions.

Willis (1866) believed that they were north-west of the Lady Chapel, but that another pair on the south side marked 'Arthur's grave'. Other writers placed them in a west–east line 8m (26ft) south of the church; this location is, however, neither close to the church, nor is one further away than the other. Ralegh Radford believed that he had located them in the 1950s, in one of his trenches south of the Lady Chapel, or at least the holes from which they had been removed. All these locations are shown in **43** and **44**.

Dunstan's cloister

One further theme represented by the archaeological evidence of the pre-Conquest features (see **43**) is the rest of the monastic layout. The cloister appears to have been rectangular, *c*.60 by 40m (197 by 130ft). Rooms of a narrow East Range were found as light foundations similar in construction to those of the phase 4 church; the walls were plastered in a cream colour; there may have been two storeys in this range. Traces of similar walls were found extending westwards (the south range), and some of the west range. There was no north range; the limit here was set by the southern wall of the cemetery (see below).

This claustral layout is one of the earliest to be found in England. Such an arrangement, though familiar from later monasteries, was not seen in Europe before the later eighth century. The best known example is that in the Plan of St Gall, a parchment plan of *c*.820 which still survives in the monastery of St Gall, in Switzerland. The reform movement spread from Europe to England during the tenth century, and Glastonbury represents one of its earliest expressions in monastic layout. It has been suggested that the well-known layout at Canterbury (where Dunstan became primate after his abbacy at Glastonbury) was based on that at Glastonbury.

Industrial activity in the Abbey

The role of the monasteries as centres of technical development is one of the most interesting aspects of the life of such communities. Together with monastic skills in agriculture, water engineering and estate management, craft activities now attract the attention of economic and art historians in addition to the more traditional interests of ecclesiastical and architectural matters.

A tantalizing glimpse of the potential of the archaeology of the Abbey to provide very important evidence in this field is afforded by a few finds made in the excavations. Even the little that is known is unique in the archaeology of Anglo-Saxon monasteries, and is thus worth describing in detail.

Significantly, the most important finds are associated with the late Saxon period. They could all be associated with Dunstan, who as well as being a religious leader was also known for his personal skills in craft (p.43). At Glastonbury, he is said to have made a gong (or bell struck like a gong) for Ina's church.

A relatively minor early find, probably of medieval date, was made in the area west of the cloisters; oyster shells were found here that had been used as palettes for colour work (perhaps for frescoes). There were residues of pigments of vermilion, azure, black and neutral colours.

In the area south of the refectory (see **42**), there was part of a heavily burnt floor and part of a flat bun-shaped ingot of bronze, with late Saxon pottery. Outside the west wall of the dorter range was further evidence of a similar kind – rough stone settings, also burnt.

Of outstanding importance were, however, features and residues associated with glassmaking. These were found in the area west of the *vallum* (see **44**). One of the glass furnaces comprised an oval hollow *c.*125 by 90cm (50 by 35in) dug into the natural clay. In and around this there was solidified ashy floor material and fragments of burnt clay (daub) from a domed superstructure. These incorporated many fragments of reused Roman brick and tile (*tegulae* and *imbrices* – from roofing). Some of the clay was vitrified (with a glassy surface) or had bubbles of molten glass adhering. Some of the Roman tile fragments also had glass adhering of a deep turquoise colour; there were crucibles with greenish-blue residues.

The whole complex shows signs of great heat. The remains of another furnace (or possibly two) were later found nearby; traces of three successive floors were also noted in this area. It appeared that the furnaces were broken up after each firing and then remade. One yielded little evidence of glass, and may have been a kiln or oven, for other stages of the work.

A variety of glass products was being made, including vessels, beads and window glass. Colours include bluish-green, deep turquoise and emerald green. Some pieces were identified as those attached to the blowing iron. There were also some that were the residues of coloured or opaque white trails applied to vessels, and one with maroon stripes. It is at present uncertain whether glass was actually being made on the site from raw materials (sand etc.) but it seems more likely that scrap glass ('cullet') was being reused. It is clear that these finds represent a considerable workshop, probably producing glass for windows, vessels for ritual or personal use, material used to decorate jewellery, reliquaries, vessels or books, and beads.

The dating of these items is provided in two ways. Firstly, the furnaces were stratified below a layer containing twelfth-century pottery. Secondly, the glass fragments can be dated by analogy with other material to the late ninth or tenth century. The glass-working is perhaps of the period of rebuilding and monastic reform associated in the middle years of the tenth century with Dunstan, who, as we have seen, was skilled in craft techniques.

While there is a lot of Roman glass, and Kentish or Rhineland glass from the great Anglo-Saxon cemeteries of eastern England in the sixth to seventh centuries, the only early post-Roman evidence for glass-making is that of a small group of crucibles with opaque white and yellow glass in them from Buckden (Northamptonshire); and melted glass ('cullet') from several Dark Age sites in the west of Britain.

Glass itself is rare in later Anglo-Saxon times. In monastic contexts, we know from written sources that glaziers were sent for from Gaul for the seventh- to eighth-century monastic foundations in the north-east. Glass has been found at a number of sites including Bede's own monastery of Jarrow, and from York Minster. There is a little window glass from late Saxon town sites such as Southampton, and pottery with vitrified coatings from York. There is also some fine glass from high-status sites at Brandon (Suffolk); Barking Abbey (Essex); and Flixborough (South Humberside). But Glastonbury is unique in having the remains of actual furnaces or ovens.

The final industrial activity recorded is that of iron-making. Eight smiths were attached to the Glastonbury Manor in Domesday Book (1086); the only archaeological evidence for this craft was found not in the Abbey precinct but at some distance to the west, at the Mound (p.138).

The Abbey precinct before the Norman Conquest

> . . . a monastery walled round and embattled like a town, a mile in compass

> *William Stukeley, eighteenth century*

Glastonbury is one of the few abbeys where something can be said of the precinct, the enclosure within which lay the nucleus of the church and monastic buildings. There would have been an inner enclosure, with many buildings; workshops for industrial activities such as those described above, together with smithies and tilers; agricultural storage and processing facilities; mills; fishponds; orchards, and vegetable and herb gardens.

Written sources indicate something of the range of buildings and activities to be expected. The layout of a monastery can look quite urban, as seen as early as the ninth century in the plan of St Gall. Only in a few places, such as Bordesley Abbey, has much archaeological exploration been done beyond the claustral buildings.

The size and character of the enclosure will have varied through the nine centuries or more of the Abbey's existence. For the pre-Conquest monastery, the boundary of the precinct is sometimes known as the *vallum monasterii*, often referred to in saints' *Lives*. Such a boundary is seen, especially in the early days of the Church, as that of the *Civitas Dei*, the city of God, separating the religious from the secular area. The *vallum* can take the form of a ditch, usually with a bank inside; or a wall of stone, turf or clay; or even a quickset hedge. Such boundaries have been located in excavations at famous sites such as Iona and Whitby; and substantial walls still enclose the great Irish monasteries such as Clonmacnoise.

The idea refers back to the desert foundations of the early monasteries in Egypt, where the boundary was a substantial wall, similar to that of city or castle. Such a limit might be constructed especially for a monastic foundation, or may have utilised an existing boundary. At Burgh Castle, St Fursey's monastery was inside the wall of a later Roman fort, and even earlier earthworks could be used. Isolation could also be secured by founding a monastery on an island such as Skellig Michael, off the coast of Kerry, Ireland.

At Glastonbury such a boundary has been suggested in several places, defining areas of greater or lesser extent. Later pages (chapter 9) discuss the possibility of a great monastic estate comprising the 'Twelve Hides', with daughter-houses set around the nucleus on the peninsula itself. A smaller area may be delineated by the earthwork known as Ponter's Ball (p.26) which runs across the causeway linking the peninsula to the 'mainland' to the east. The sixth-century foundation on the Tor, if indeed an early monastic foundation, needed no enclosing bank to reinforce its precipitous slopes (p.67).

Within the town, major enclosures extended from the hill slope behind the Abbey to St Benignus' church, changing through time; this 'precinct' will be discussed later. What appears to be part of this enclosure around the monastery buildings and their immediate vicinity was located within the Abbey grounds.

To the east of the pre-Conquest churches, a ditch with an internal (westerly) bank was located by excavation in three places (see **44**). Sections were drawn where this bank was found below the later chapter house and north transept; they are redrawn here in a simpler form (**62**).

There was no dating evidence in the bank, or under it in the earlier ground surface; this suggests that the *vallum* is here a primary feature of the Abbey complex; the ditch fill was also barren of artefacts. An important facet of the ditch excavation which was not exploited was the high degree of survival of organic debris in the ditch fill: 'soft and peaty, with vegetable matter, leaves and twigs'. Today this would be an invaluable source of environmental evidence (pollen, beetles, molluscs etc.) and dating for pre-Conquest Glastonbury.

The *vallum* thus located in the Abbey grounds must be seen as an element in the earliest layout, forming at least one eastern boundary to the complex of churches *c*.50m (165ft) to the west. The present limit of the precinct, within which part of the east side of the *vallum* was found, marks the final medieval

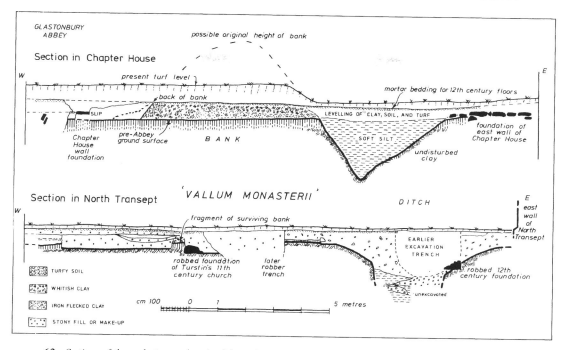

62 *Sections of the enclosing earthwork of the early monastery – the* vallum monasterii, *as recorded by C.A. Ralegh Radford. This consisted of a bank (possibly with a fence on top), and a ditch on its outer side.* After Radford, 1981

and later definition of the Abbey grounds as distinct from the town outside (see below, p.127). It is not known how far the line defined in the excavated area continued to the north and south, nor where the other three sides lie.

Outside the Abbey grounds, intensive redevelopment of properties in the last decade has necessitated several excavations. In these, numerous ditches and other features have been located, with some Saxon radiocarbon dates. These indicate the complexity of changes in the precinct boundary, and their relationship to the medieval town. Suggested reconstructions of the plan of the precinct at different periods are shown in **63** and **64**.

The precinct in medieval times

In the twelfth century, there were radical changes to the precinct boundary, and also to some extent to its function. While still enclosing the monastic complex, it also now served as a framework for the systematic creation and development of the town; such urban enterprise by both secular and ecclesiastical authorities is well known at this time.

These changes, associated with Abbots Turstin and Herlewin, have been seen as 'signifying the stamp of Norman authority on what had been one of the principal

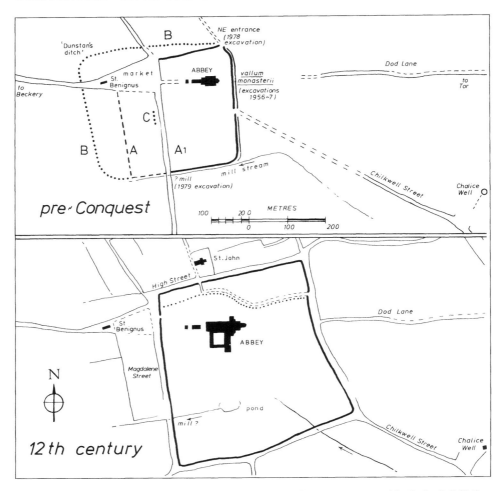

63 *The plan of the Abbey precinct before and after the Norman Conquest as suggested by Rodwell (1984). It will be seen that the precinct acts as a focus for many of the roads converging on Glastonbury.* After Rodwell, 1984

religious and monastic centres of Anglo-Saxon England'. Excavation in 1988 located a large ditch of this date, extending west to east between Silver Street and High Street (**65**); this is likely to be the post-Conquest north side of the precinct, incorporating the north gatehouse (see **64**).

The present precinct stone wall dates from the fifteenth century. Much of it has been demolished, but long stretches still remain. In places it has been examined by excavation; only the lower courses are likely to be of medieval date.

The area underwent many changes in internal divisions and boundaries between medieval times and the present day. These are recorded on various maps from 1625 down to the time of the Ordnance Survey and include various alterations to the area and extent of the market in the north-west corner.

The interior of the precinct

After over 1,000 years of religious and secular activity focused on the Abbey, it is hardly surprising that the precinct is a highly complex site. Only excavation can reveal the full details of the successive monastic buildings and other features, and the use made of the area after the Dissolution. Something can be said, however, on the basis of non-destructive survey – of earthworks and parchmarks which appeared in the dry summer of 1989 (**66**).

The earthworks consist of banks, hollows, scarps, terraces and silted-up ditches – all the marks of human earth-moving in the past. The parchmarks, where the grass has largely died and turned brown or yellow, indicate the presence of sub-surface features which inhibit the nourishment of grass roots. Some are clearly the foundations of buildings; others may be stony areas such as courtyards or metalling; dumps of stony material from building or excavation; or excavation trenches back-filled with largely sterile material such as clay. The survey located dozens of new features. The work indicates what a rich harvest lies in store for the archaeologists of the future.

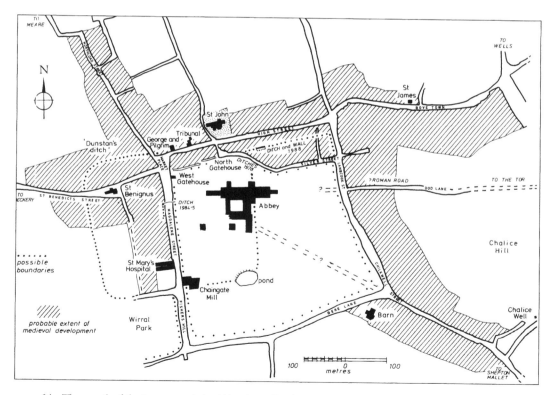

64 *The growth of the town around the Abbey in medieval times. Note the location of the Abbey Barn, Chalice Well, and the deer park of Wirral.* After Burrow, Ellis, Holingrake, Leech and Rodwell

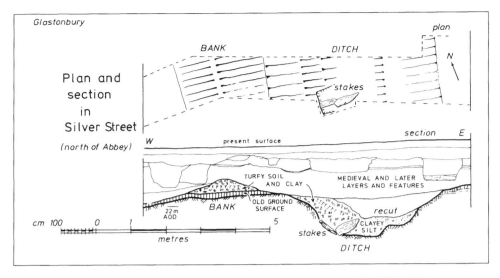

65 *Section of the post-Conquest north enclosure ditch, found in Silver Street. After Ellis, 1982*

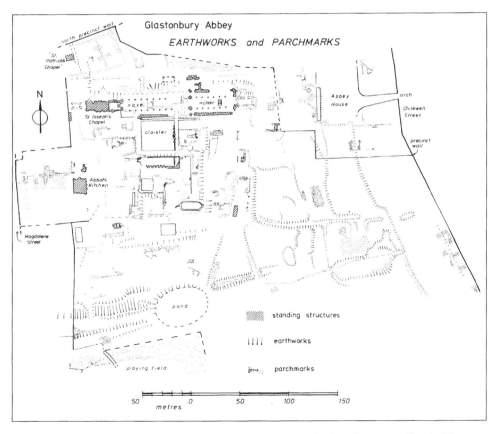

66 *Earthworks and parchmarks as seen in the precinct in 1989 by Charles and Nancy Hollinrake. This shows how much remains to be discovered in areas that have not been excavated.*
After N. and C. Hollinrake, 1989

The southern earthworks and mill

The earthworks in the southern part of the area (**67**) are interpreted as a fishpond or mill-pond complex, defined by an artificial dam, and presumably fed by water from springs in the Chalice Hill area and from Chalice Well (medieval *Chalcewelle*) after 1184. This is merely part of what must have been a complex water system of the Abbey. Water would have been necessary not only for fishponds and mill-power but for use in the Abbey itself, for drinking, cooking, washing and the flushing of lavatories. It would have been systematically channelled and piped in a system of decreasing purity, as elsewhere.

The fishpond was later drained, the water being led to a second pond, still existing, which is not medieval in its present form. Further west, other earthworks were also associated with water-management, leading to the mill. The earthworks include rectangular terraced enclosures, perhaps for vegetable or herb beds or gardens.

The nineteenth-century Chaingate Flour Mills were demolished in 1979. Excavations showed that there had been two ponds, with a dam in between. The ponds were silted up by the thirteenth century, and are thus possibly associated with a mill in this area, of Anglo-Saxon or early medieval date.

These surveys have provided a framework for future studies through technically advanced methods, which predict what is below the ground without actually digging.

The Abbey garden

Survey or excavation can sometimes suggest the location of horticultural areas, or such details as bedding trenches. In favourable conditions (such as a waterlogged,

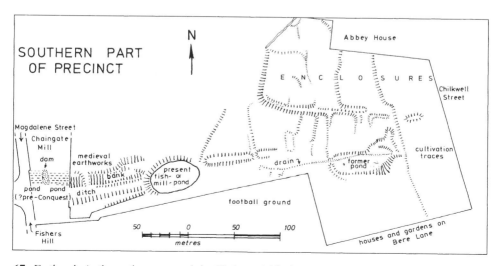

67 *Earthworks in the southern area, and the Chaingate Mill, close to Magdalene Street (see **64**).*

anaerobic environment), seeds or pollen can indicate what was growing nearby, but a full record is beyond the reach of these techniques.

Fortunately there exists a written source which tells us a great deal about the Abbey garden at one point in time – in the 1330s, a decade before the Black Death. The document is a cash account of the Abbey gardener at this time, one Thomas of Keynsham. Its purpose was to record purchases and sales of garden produce.

The gardens included an orchard, a vineyard, a herb garden, vegetable plots, possibly some flower beds and pasture. Cash receipts for 1333-4 (Michaelmas to Michaelmas) were £4 6s 5½d. The sales or issues were of herbage and nettles, income from grazing and garden produce. The latter included three tuns of cider, linen (from flax), hemp, onions, garlic, madder and linseed plants, leek plants, pears and apples. Other income came from the sale of brushwood, mixed grain, old spade irons (the metal tips of wooden spades) and a horse.

The gardener spent money on seeds for beans and hemp, wages for helpers, and payments to a smith for repair to tools and fittings. Ten moles were captured, and 3d paid for these. Four pairs of gloves and some tools were also bought; the latter included a sickle, an axe, five spades and four hoes.

The vineyard is of special interest: it supplied 105 gallons of verjuice (unfermented). There were also vineyards on the southern slopes of Wirral Hill. Grapes were being grown on the manor as early as 1086 (Domesday Book). Madder could be used for rennet or for dye. Also surprising is the amount of garlic: 11,000 cloves in this year – 2,000 of these went to the Abbot's kitchen, and 6,000 to the 'larderer' for the use of the inn.

There are also details in this account of fruit and other material bought from outside Glastonbury, from manors or estates (p.147) and the destinations for the produce – the Abbey itself, local hospitality or more distant manors.

This evocative account reminds us that in the Middle Ages, at least, the Abbey was a highly organised capitalist institution, with full accounting; its primary identity as providing the infrastructure of a major order would not have survived except on such a well-regulated economic basis.

Daily life at the Abbey

The last section indicates something of the organization of the Abbey's productivity. To this may be added some of the sparse detail available on the life of the monks themselves, outside their primary duties of worship and liturgical observations. Two accounts at either end of the medieval period are selected, in the twelfth and sixteenth centuries.

The first is included in the text of William of Malmesbury, concerning customs. Diet was normally austere, but:

on holy days the brethren had cups of mead, fine wheaten cakes on the table, and a measure of wine; more was made available on special feast days. Each of the monks was to have two cowls, two frocks, two shirts of linsey-woolsey, two pairs of breeches, four pairs of stockings and a new pelisse [mantle] every year; and on Maundy Thursday each was to have two shoes for the day time (and in winter for the night), and two bed-covers.

A further document of 1248 (a letter from Pope Innocent IV to the Archbishop of Canterbury) recounts that the abbot and monks petition:

> that as their monastery is built in a cold place, it is dangerous for them to attend services bare-headed; they ask to be allowed to use their skull-caps. The Archbishop is to allow them their request.

The second account comes from the accounts submitted to Henry VIII at the time of the Dissolution.

> Extra food was provided during Advent and Lent; on the Monday after Advent... pea soup and fresh fish . . . on the Tuesday vegetable soup and fritters fried in oil, on Wednesday fish soup flavoured with pepper, cinnamon, raisins and mustard.

There were four stills:

> where cordials and liqueurs were produced for the sick; the latter, especially after blood-letting, needed great quantities of oats for porridge, butter, milk, fresh fish, ginger, cinnamon, geese, pasties and joints of meat.

On the occasion of the feast of the dedication of the church, the cook supplied:

> corn, gruel, milk, sugar, pepper and saffron, twelve sucking pigs and three pounds of large raisins. On Lady Day . . . six salted salmon with sugar, pepper and saffron; on Easter Day six lambs and a quantity of Easter eggs; on Corpus Christi Day meat pasties, spices and malted barley.

In the last quarter of 1538, consumption was recorded of: 56 quarters of bread, 90 oxen, 3 cows, 1 bull, 146 sheep, 6 calves, 7 pigs, 62 pigs' trotters, 174 pounds of butter, 11 stone of cheese, salt fish including 381 cod, 290 hake, 18 salmon and 497 white herrings; and 27,000 bundles of firewood.

Conclusion

In this chapter the evidence for the early history and archaeology of the Abbey and its precinct has been described. No finds or other datable material have been recovered which would show that the Abbey site was developed as a monastery before the seventh century. Such Roman finds as have been found are not associated with any of the early structures, and it is unlikely that they are in any way to be associated with a Christian use of the site. There are, indeed, no finds from the Abbey excavations which can be dated to the seventh century, let alone the fifth or sixth; any theory of a substantial or long British Christian presence must be argued from the very difficult written sources.

There is a find from the Abbey area, however, which may be associated with at least the seventh century. This is a remarkable leaded brass censer (**68**) – a device to hold burning incense, swung around on its chain to spread the fumes around the church. This example is of Byzantine origin – a rare find in Britain – and would have been made in the Eastern Mediterranean in the late sixth to mid-seventh century. It was found in the early 1980s, though not unfortunately either in controlled excavation, or in the Abbey precinct. It probably came from the Silver Street area to the north (see **64**) where deep excavations for road works were in progress at that time. There is, of course, no knowing how it got to Glastonbury, or how old it was when it was in use there. It is, however, a rare and expensive object and could have been a gift to the Abbey by a king or someone else of high status.

This chapter has only touched on the complex medieval history of the Abbey, culminating in its violent end and progressive destruction. That anything remains at all is fortunate; we owe the survival of the splendid Abbot's kitchen (**colour plate 26**) to the use of it by Flemish weavers in the later sixteenth century; and later as a Quaker Meeting House. In our own day, what remains is safe and should survive for many centuries if it is properly cared for.

68 *Leaded brass censer (a device to hold burning incense); this was made somewhere in the Eastern Mediterranean in the sixth or seventh century. It was found in the early 1980s near Silver Street*

8

THE MEDIEVAL TOWN
AND ITS ENVIRONS

This chapter discusses the medieval town, and what are now its suburbs. There are in this area a number of fine buildings associated with the Abbey, and also, further to the south-east the archaeologically important features of Chalice Well and the Mound.

Townscape and traders

It was emphasised in chapter 7 that the development of the Abbey precinct reflected the separation of ecclesiastical from extramural, secular interests. At the same time it provided a framework for urban development under the authority of the abbots, a process becoming more positively authoritarian in Norman times. The boundary of the precinct changed through time, firstly as the Abbey itself expanded its range of buildings, and later as increasingly the town encroached on the precinct, especially in the centuries after the Dissolution. The enveloping of the precinct by the medieval urban properties is illustrated in **64**, which also shows the ribbon development along the roads to the north, east and south-east.

Urbanism at Glastonbury was initiated in late Saxon times, by the development of services catering for the needs of the Abbey, and dependent on its fortunes. It was never, however, a town in any formal sense before the Conquest: it never had a mint, nor is it described as a town in Domesday Book.

The principal development of the town was in the twelfth to thirteenth centuries. The core of the medieval development was outside the north-west corner of the precinct, approached by way of the north and west gatehouses. Here was a market-place. Originally this had an octagonal market cross, similar to those surviving in the county at Shepton Mallet and Dunster. To the north, in High Street, were important medieval buildings, both secular (the George and Pilgrim Inn) and ecclesiastical (the parish church of St John).

Further west was a separate nucleus around the church of St Benignus. There was probably a secondary market-place here. South of this, Magdalene Street was built up on its west side, the east side being the precinct boundary. To the east, development extended up the hill of Bove Town, where there was a medieval chapel of St James. Properties extended south of this area along the east side of

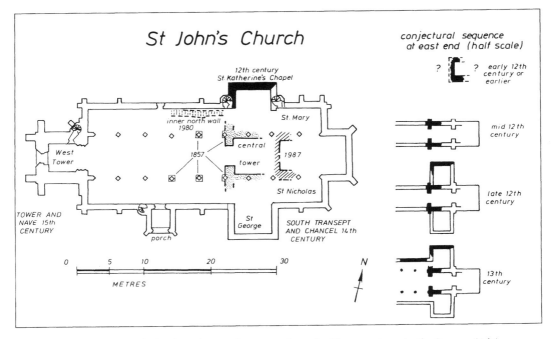

69 *St John's Church; this has been shown to have a complex earlier history, as shown by the diagrams (right).* After N. and C. Hollinrake, 1980, 1987

Lambcook Street, and beyond around the Abbey Barn and Chilkwell Street down to the area by what is now Chalice Well.

Most of the streets date from the thirteenth century: High Street, Northload Street, St Benedict's Street, Magdalene Street, Chilkwell Street, Doddlene (Dod Lane), Cock Lane and *Gropecuntlene* are all mentioned in deeds of this period. The evocative last name is found also in Bristol and York. Cock Lane was one of the few areas licensed for prostitution in the fourteenth century. Tenements are also recorded as being built in the early thirteenth century; occupations named in 1203 include bakers, launderers, master porters, cooks, goldsmiths, butlers and reeves; pilgrims would have been a useful source of revenue. By 1319, two burgesses represented Glastonbury in Parliament.

Not surprisingly, most of the medieval buildings have been demolished and replaced; but several have survived largely unchanged, in remarkably good condition. They are, of course, of stone, and so have survived better than those built of wood or clay.

St John

This church is sometimes known as St John the Baptist or St John Northbin (**69**). It is the parish church, a notable landmark with its 41m (135ft) high tower, the

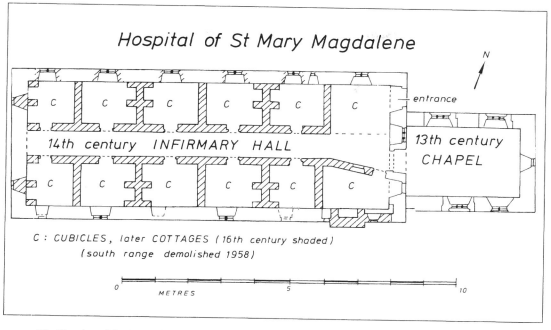

70 *The plan of the Hospital, with cubicles on either side of an infirmary hall, and a chapel at the east end*

second highest in the county. The earliest written reference is in 1175. The oldest extant part is the north chapel of St Katherine, of the twelfth century. The south transept (St George's Chapel) and east end are of fourteenth-century work. The church originally had a central tower, but this collapsed about 1465. The part of the church west of this, the nave and western tower, are of the later fifteenth century.

Excavations have exposed foundations or foundation trenches earlier than anything now standing. In 1857 the foundations of much of the central tower of the late twelfth or early thirteenth century were uncovered, showing that St John had originally been a cruciform church. In 1980 the foundation trench for the former north wall of the nave was located; this allowed the tentative reconstructions on the right of **69** to be drawn out by the Hollinrakes.

In 1987 the foundations of a narrower structure at the west end of the chancel were located, at a greater depth than those found in 1857. It is suggested that this could be part of a previous church, of the earlier twelfth century, or even pre-Conquest; these foundations had destroyed even earlier burials. The church of St John may thus have an earlier origin than has been supposed. It could belong to the earliest stages of development of the town, as a place of worship for the growing number of people who were not members of the monastic community. Such churches were often founded outside the gates of monastic institutions.

In many places, the monastic church was taken over by the townspeople after the Dissolution, and used as a parish church, usually reduced in size. This did not happen at Glastonbury, presumably because St John's was adequate for the urban population, who in any case had lost part of their livelihood after the Abbey was abandoned.

St Benignus (now St Benedict)

This church is at the west end of the town, 150m (500ft) west of the main market place. This area is close to the western approaches to Glastonbury, by way of the River Brue (see pp.141-4). It is also near the postulated end of the canal (p.144), the market-place being its terminus. St Benignus was an early saint. Two translations of his bones are recorded. The first was in a shrine box given by King Harthacnut to the Abbey in 1040. In 1091, the bones were brought by boat from Meare; this was the supposed occasion for the church being built at this spot, under Abbot Turstin.

Nothing as early as this is to be seen in the present building, and no excavation has taken place here. It is worth noting, however, that the church is on the same west–east axis that includes the Abbey (p.90).

The earliest surviving part, the chancel, is fourteenth century, but the rest, including the tower, is the work of Abbot Bere, in the early sixteenth century; his initials can be seen on the north porch, on a roof-corner in the north aisle, and on the tower.

Other surviving medieval buildings

Other medieval buildings that survive include the west gatehouse of the Abbey; almshouses and hospitals with their associated chapels; a fine inn; the building known as the 'Tribunal'; and, most impressively, the Abbey Barn.

The west gatehouse of the Abbey opens onto Market Street, and survives almost intact in its late medieval form. There are two entrances, one for vehicles and one for pedestrians. The gatehouse now forms the entrance for visitors to the Abbey. St James' Chapel or 'Jacoby Cottage' (no. 7 Bove Town) was a medieval pilgrimage chapel, now converted into a cottage, though one three-light window survives.

St Patrick's Almshouses are incorporated in the Abbey grounds by the main gatehouse. Little remains of the hall and domestic buildings themselves, but the chapel survives (with the original altar), and is now used as a place of private prayer (St Patrick's Chapel). This complex was built by Abbot Bere in 1517 for women, but an earlier version is known to have existed as early as 1246.

St Mary's Almshouses (or the Hospital of St Mary Magdalene) (**70** & **colour plate 12**) is a most interesting and attractive group of buildings, set back on the west side of Magdalene Street. It is a quiet retreat from the bustle of the street. Until relatively recently it consisted of two ranges of little cottages facing each other, with a chapel at the east end, but the south side was demolished in 1958.

The whole was built as an almshouse for poor men under a master in the thirteenth century, moved here in 1251 from the north side of St John's Church. Originally there was a long infirmary hall with cubicles on either side. In the sixteenth century the hall roof was destroyed and the cubicles converted into cottages. The chapel is mostly of thirteenth century date. A stone bell-turret is of the fourteenth century; in a niche on the gable is a statue of St Mary Magdalene, standing on a corbel, which is carved with a girl's head.

The George and Pilgrim Inn (High Street) (71) is one of the best of the surviving pre-Reformation inns in the country, and still affords fine food and beer for the weary archaeologist, as it did for the medieval pilgrims. It was built by Abbot Selwood about 1450 and is of three storeys in stone. The façade on to the

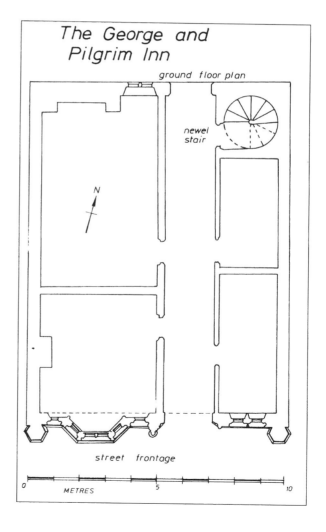

71 *The George and Pilgrim Inn, plan of the ground floor*

street resembles a small castle, with battlements; much medieval stone and wooden panelling survive inside, including a fine newel stair. A total of 95 other taverns are recorded in medieval times.

The Tribunal (High Street) was once thought to have been the Court House, in which the abbot administered justice (**72** & **73**). It dates from the fifteenth century, with a new front built by Abbot Bere around 1500. The name is not, however, known before 1791, and the building has now been shown to have been a substantial merchant's house. It is of two storeys, with a separate kitchen block at the back; it was a school in the early nineteenth century.

In 1982, the Tribunal was acquired by the then Department of Environment, who restored it. It is now an attractive small museum administered by English Heritage. It houses the collections of the Glastonbury Antiquarian Society (p.163), mainly of the 'Lake Village' finds (p.26) (though most of these are in the County Museum at Taunton Castle).

The Abbey Barn (colour plates 27 & 28)

The most complete and splendid of all surviving medieval buildings in Glastonbury is the Abbey Barn; it lies close to the south-east corner of the walled area of the Abbey (**74-6**). It is one of four surviving fine barns built to store rendered produce (p.146) from the abbey estates, the others being at Doulting, Pilton and West Bradley (**77**).

The barn is over 28m (92ft) long and 10m (33ft) wide, with extensions to the south-east and north-west. There are seven bays, with central cart-porches. These have wagon entrances in limestone; the roof is of graduated stone slates, weighing in total over 80 tonnes.

Below the windows in the main gables are carved emblems of the four evangelists; St Luke, as a winged bull; St John, as an eagle, St Mark, as a winged lion; and St Matthew, as a winged man. The main gables are topped by figures of the Virgin Mary and a bishop.

The barn is usually ascribed to Abbot Bere, in the sixteenth century: it used to be said that his arms were carved on the building, but this is incorrect. Recent work on the medieval roof timbers used dendrochronological (tree-ring) dating, and showed that the trees used were felled in 1343-61. It is possible that this was not in fact the original roof, but a replacement: there are records of a thatched barn at Glastonbury as early as 1302; the building as we see it today is unlikely, from the architectural style, to be earlier than the fourteenth century. The porch roofs were replaced with new timbers in 1976-7; the barn is now part of the Somerset Rural Life Museum (below, p.167). When offered for sale in 1850 it was suggested that it would be 'entirely convertible into a public or private chapel', but it stayed as a farm building until given to Somerset County Council in 1974.

72 *The Tribunal when it was a day school, in the early nineteenth century*

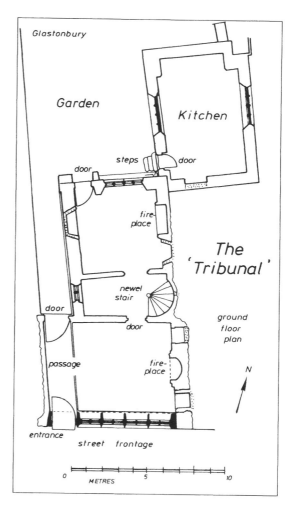

73 *The Tribunal: plan of the ground floor.*
After HMSO Guide

133

74 *The Abbey Barn, western porch from the south-west.* Somerset County Museums Service

75 *The roof timbers of the Abbey Barn (fourteenth century).* Somerset County Museums Service

Chalice Well

The gardens of Chalice Well, lying in a sheltered cleft between Chalice Hill and the Tor, are one of the pleasantest spots in the whole of the Glastonbury area, with gardens arranged around a series of fountains and water issues. These originate from Chalice Well itself, at the upper end of the garden. To the casual visitor, this looks like a stone-lined well, complete with a wooden cover and fine wrought-iron decoration. Its present fame rests on a tradition of no great age (p.59), that this was a holy well, in which Joseph of Arimathea washed the vessels of the Passion after his arrival at Glastonbury, This has led not only to the influx of present-day pilgrims (see p.165) but to the establishment earlier in the century (1958) of the Chalice Well Trust, who now safeguard the complex for posterity.

The 'well' structure is built over a major spring, yielding some 109,000 litres (24,000 gallons) of water a day at a temperature of 11° C (52°F): the major source for the settlement on the Tor above, and later for the Abbey; and indeed for any settlement in the vicinity. The water precipitates a reddish-brown deposit which is responsible for the (recent) name of Blood Spring; a stream carries this water down to Bere Lane.

In 1961, the Trust sponsored an excavation to determine whether there was any evidence of Christian or pre-Christian use of the area, to support the idea of an early sacred site here. Flints and Roman pottery showed that the spring had been frequented in earlier times; it would have been the principal water supply for the Dark Age and Anglo-Saxon settlements on the Tor above (**colour plate 6**).

The excavation was deep; the original ground surface was reached at 4m (13ft). Near the well was the stump of a yew tree dated to the Roman period. The yew is well known for its association with Christian churchyards; it also has a sacred association in classical antiquity. A grove of yews is still growing by the Roman temple site at Pagans Hill, to the north of Mendip; and some still grow by Chalice Well today. The 'well' was demonstrated to be a hole made in the roof of a medieval well-house (**78** & **80**). This was built in the late twelfth century, after the fire of 1184, to protect the water supply at its source.

Such small buildings are well known in monastic contexts; two complete examples may be seen at Mount Grace (North Yorkshire) and one at Haughmond Abbey (Shropshire). Their function was to protect the spring from interference and pollution before it was led to and through the monastery by complex systems. The water would have been carried by gravity the 200-300m (650-1000ft) down

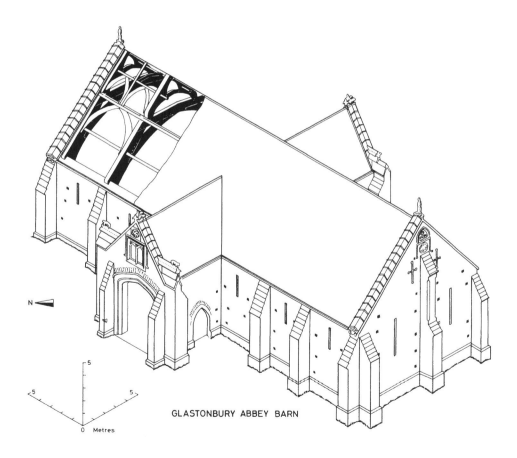

76 *Isometric drawing of the Barn*

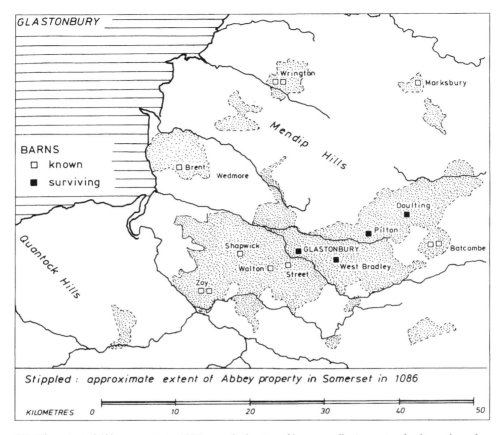

77 *The extent of Abbey property in 1086; note the location of barns as collecting centres for the produce of these estates.* After Bond and Weller, 1991

to the Abbey; wooden pipes, of hollowed-out interlocking tree segments, have been dug up from time to time on this route.

Once the well-house had been built, however, there was no longer any scouring from the spring to carry away the silt, which accordingly built up around the well-house, eventually burying it right up to the level of its roof (**79**); subsequently part of this roof was taken away, to make a well-like opening, complete with cover; this is what is now visible (**80**). The water exit will have been to the west, curving around the base of Chalice Hill towards the Abbey. It may be noted that the lane to the east is called Wellhouse Lane, but it is not known how ancient this name is.

In the medieval period, the source was known as *Chalcewelle* (1210) and *Chalkwell* (1306): this gave the name to Chilkwell Street. There is no evidence for a medieval origin for *Chalice*. In the eighteenth century, and again in the twentieth, the water acquired further reputations; discussion on these is deferred to a later chapter as are the features in the upper part of the valley.

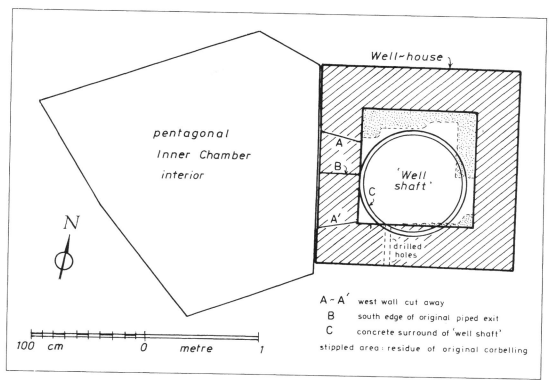

78 *Plan of the well-house, showing the position of the present 'well shaft' of Chalice Well; the later addition (left) for the eighteenth-century spa is of brick construction.* After Rahtz, 1964

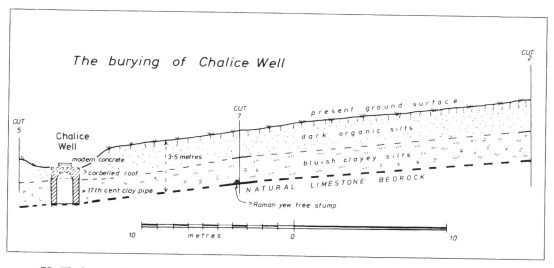

79 *The burying of Chalice Well. When there was a free-flowing spring and stream, the silt from the slopes above would have been carried away; but when the twelfth-century well-house was built, this process stopped. The well-house was buried in silt; the present Chalice Well is a hole made in its roof.* After Rahtz, 1964

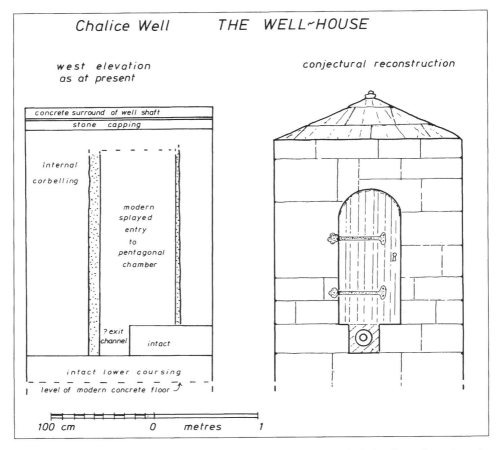

80 *The west side of the well-house as now visible below ground in the later brick chamber; and a conjectural drawing showing how it may have appeared in the twelfth to thirteenth centuries, when it protected the spring for the Abbey water-supply*

The Mound

Also known as 'The Mount' or 'Glastonbury Castle', this was an 'island' or higher area on the south-west side of the town, about a kilometre from the Abbey. It was close to Mill Lane (near the former station) and not far from Beckery and the River Brue on the western edge of the Glastonbury peninsula. It was unfortunately totally levelled in 1972 for industrial development. The raised area was 40 by 30m (130 by 100ft) in extent, and about 5m (16ft) high, above the low-lying surrounding moors. Most of the height was of natural clay, but the upper metre was a dense layer of archaeological refuse.

The mound was formerly thought to be wholly artificial. A *castellum* of Henri de Blois – a twelfth-century abbot of Glastonbury – is recorded, and it was thought that the Mound was a motte and bailey or ringwork castle; but it is now thought that the *castellum* was a semi-fortified building within the Abbey grounds.

Small excavations at various times have recovered flints, Roman pottery and some sherds of Dark Age amphorae (to be compared with those on the Tor, p.70); these indicate that some use was made of the area in earlier centuries. The Mound was a good place to take refuge when the lower-lying surrounding area was inundated by water. This site (like Beckery – see below) could also be seen as a point where pilgrims and earlier travellers to Glastonbury alighted from boats: the first landmark of raised ground on the way to the higher areas of the peninsula. The most important discoveries were, however, two iron-smelting furnaces of the tenth to twelfth centuries. This is presumably one of the iron-making sites that belonged to the Abbey in later Anglo-Saxon and Norman times; several are recorded in Domesday Book. This may be another of the 'craft' activities pioneered by Dunstan.

The location of iron-making furnaces here, rather than nearer to the Abbey, may have been because of the noxious fumes and noise of such work, and also the fire-risk. There is also the possibility that this was the unloading place for the iron ore and timber needed for the smelting and smithing. Wood would have been obtainable from the Levels; the ore may have come by boat from areas further to the north-west, where it is plentiful; or from another iron-rich area in Gloucestershire, where the Abbey owned a manor (at Pucklechurch). The products of the industry (tools, fittings, harness, animal shoes) would have been for the Abbey or its manors, A possible route to the Abbey (by water) is suggested below (p.145), The cessation of the industry may have been due to the creation of the Wirral deer park, in the thirteenth century, which effectively isolated the Mound area from town and abbey.

Surprisingly, there was also a mass of domestic refuse: over 1,000 pieces of pottery, over 5,000 animal bones, and objects of iron, copper alloy, lead, bone and baked clay. The iron includes tools: knives, saws, a chisel and a padlock, Among the copper alloy pieces is the arm of a pair of folding scales; and there are spindle-whorls of bone and clay. All this is more like the material that would come from deep urban excavation in towns like York or London; its presence here, in the apparent absence of associated structures, is difficult to explain. It is the animal bones, however, which are most surprising. Apart from the usual range of food-bones of cattle, pig and sheep or goat, there are bones of horse, donkey, cat, goose, fowl and duck; and more exotically wild animals and birds: deer, otter, beaver, swan and pelican. The latter is a rare visitor to British shores, and the beaver (known also from the Iron Age 'Lake Village' (p.26), was probably extinct by the twelfth century, due to increasing drainage of habitats.

The Mound is one of the few sites associated with the later Anglo-Saxon and early medieval Abbey, the others being wholly ecclesiastical – the monastic sites of Beckery and the Tor.

9

BEYOND GLASTONBURY

. . . an island set amidst extensive pools, surrounded by water rich in fish and by sluggish rivers

'B' Life of Dunstan

Land routes

The principal land routes to and from Glastonbury are three in number. To the north the main link was to the major ecclesiastical and urban centre of Wells, with which Glastonbury's own history is entwined. The original route (**81**) was via Bove Town (the present Wells Road was constructed after 1782). Either route had to traverse 2-3km (1-2 miles) of watery moor, by way of a raised causeway. The second approach is the only one possible by continuous dry land, from the east. This connects with the 'mainland' in the Shepton Mallet area, through Ponter's Ball.

The third route to the south is of some antiquity. This linked Glastonbury with the heartland of Somerset: Somerton and beyond, and to the Polden Hills ridgeway and the estuary of the River Parrett. The first stage was a causeway linking Glastonbury to Street. The latter name may imply that this was a 'hard road' in earlier centuries; this name can also imply a Roman origin.

Street is linked with Glastonbury's early history in connection with St Kai, dating to about AD 700, at Lantokai (p.35). In the Saxon and medieval periods, Street would have been the nearest source for the easily-quarried Lias limestone, used extensively in Glastonbury; so this road had to be substantial enough for use by pack-horses.

The causeway had to cross some 600m (2,000ft) of low-lying land, the small valley of the River Brue. The earliest (pre-medieval) version of the road was found in the fields, 12m (40ft) to the east of the present road. John Morland, seeing a parchmark here at the end of the last century, found a causeway under the turf. This consisted of a layer of stones set on brushwood, held in place by upright piles. Some heavy oak timbers were found a few metres from the River Brue.

This more substantial construction may have been part of a wooden bridge-head. Street Bridge stood here (named as such as early as 1163), and a mill that

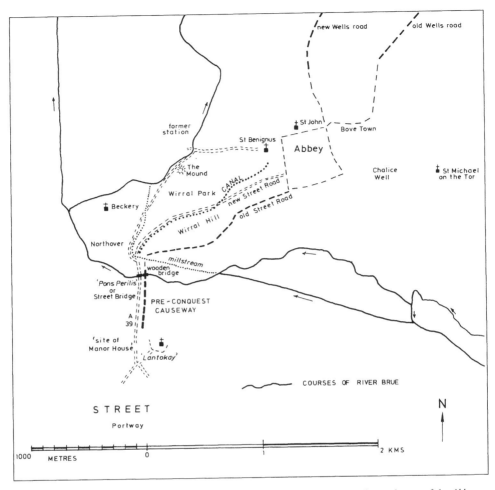

81 *The focal point of routes by land and water is the crossing of the river Brue, to the south-west of the Abbey.* After S.C. Morland

belonged to the Abbey kitchen was adjacent; this would presumably be the destination of the causewayed road of medieval and later date (now the A39), over the present stone two-arched bridge.

Later in the thirteenth century, the abbots made a great improvement. The Brue was embanked, a mill-stream cut and a new mill was set up at Beckery that had an adequate supply of water. The causeway was replaced by a new road with a stone bridge with two arches that came to be called Pomparles, a name probably derived from *pons periculosus*, the 'dangerous bridge' of Arthurian legend. Indeed it is named *Pons Perilis* on the present Ordnance Survey map. Leland used this name in the sixteenth century.

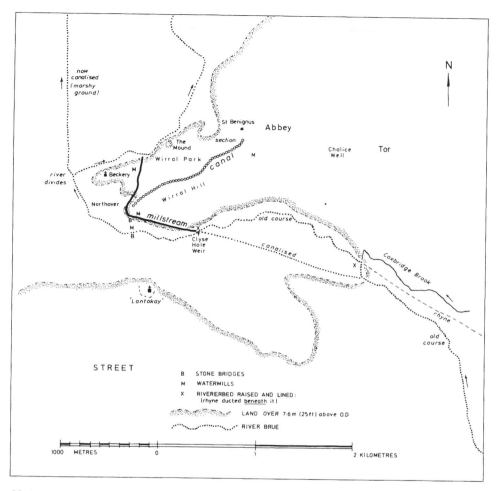

82 *Water systems were based on management of the River Brue and various springs. They provided means of transport for people and material, and a source of power for watermills. The water had to be carefully controlled to minimise flooding.* After S.C. Morland

Having crossed the Brue, the road crossed the mill-stream by a stone bridge at Northover into the town, then turned eastward along the southern slopes of Wirral Hill as the 'Old Street Road', now Roman Way.

Water routes

The western approaches by water, from the Bristol Channel and beyond, by way of the River Brue, in its natural and altered courses, have been discussed already in several places in this book. Successive abbots developed the navigation systems which led from the coast to Glastonbury. These were of considerable importance to the Abbey for local transport and not surprisingly there were officials and tenants charged with water management. There are numerous written references to this, including the duty of one thirteenth-century tenant to provide a boat big enough to carry eight men. He was responsible for 'carrying the abbot and his men, the cook, the huntsmen and his dogs, wherever they wished to, and could, travel by water; for carrying letters to outlying manors, and wine from the vineyards at Panborough (see **84**), carefully guarded, to Glastonbury'.

Apart from the transport of fish and eels from Meare Pool and the fish weirs, and other supplies from coastal areas, a major item was the carrying of brushwood for warming and cooking at the Abbey. This had to be provided and carried by the tenants at Baltonsborough, Butleigh, Street, Shapwick and Walton. The nucleus of the water transport system was the River Brue. In its long course through central Somerset, it flows along the south side of the Glastonbury peninsula, separating it from Street. It then traverses the Somerset Levels, finally reaching the Bristol Channel at Highbridge.

In its present course around Glastonbury, it has been considerably altered (**82**). The straight stretch above Clyse Hole was built up, not dug, with tree trunks on the peat for a foundation, as was seen when the weir above Clyse Hole was rebuilt. Above the tree trunks was a mass of clay to make a river bottom and sides. The water level in the river is up to 60cm (24in) above the surface of the fields on either side. The most important underpass is at Clyse Hole: it takes the water from

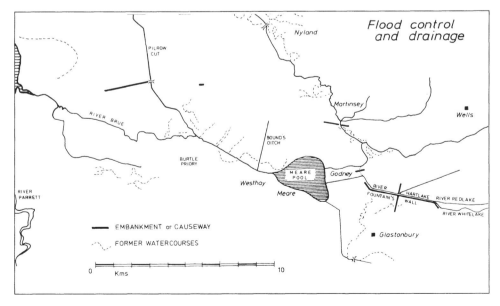

83 *The water courses around Glastonbury, extending westwards to the coast, were controlled by embankments and canalization, to facilitate drainage and prevent flooding.* After Williams, 1970

the old course of the Brue, under the Mill Street, into the old course again towards Street Bridge. Before this was done, the Brue, below Street Bridge, split into two arms which also rejoined further north. After the Dissolution the management of waterways became a responsibility of Quarter Sessions; systematic control was not re-established until comparatively recent times (**83**).

The canal (82)

The only ancient feature of the water system that has been examined archaeologically is what is probably a canal, over 2m (6ft) deep. This ran along the contours on the north side of Wirral Hill from Glastonbury to Northover, a distance of nearly 2km (over a mile); water would enter it from sources near the Abbey and drain out at Northover. The upcast from the digging of it was piled on the north-west side. On this, as noted above, the present road was built. The silted canal itself is still visible in places along the south-east side of the road, as grass-covered hollows. Excavations were undertaken by the Hollinrakes in 1986-7, in advance of the construction of supermarkets and car parks in this area (formerly the medieval deer park of Wirral; and more recently the Fair Field).

Radiocarbon dates from wood found suggest a late Anglo-Saxon date for the canal. If this dating is correct it would be unique, the earliest in Britain by some four centuries (apart from Roman examples). It would have been useful, at this time, for the movement of goods in and out of the town, from and to the navigable waterways beyond Northover; and for the transporting of pilgrims and visitors from the river to the Abbey. Notably, there would be a cost saving 'if packhorses carrying building stone from Street were saved the last part of their journey by off-loading into a boat at Northover' (Morland 1991).

A second possibility is that the canal was associated with the watermills in the thirteenth century and later. If the water filled slowly from the Glastonbury end, it could be released into the millstream above Beckery to provide additional power for the mill there. The Chaingate Mill in Glastonbury (which may only have been established after 1539) must have relied on water from Bushy Combe and Chalice Well, possibly inadequate while the Abbey was using water. This water would have been directed into the canal.

The final possibility is that it was a long fishpond, fed by water at the Glastonbury end. Fishponds are a common feature at monastic sites to provide an accessible source of fresh fish (by netting); but none is known of this length.

Between the thirteenth century (when Wirral Park was created) and the Dissolution, it would have been wholly within the park, which included both this flatter area, the crest of Wirral Hill and the southern slopes as far as the old road from Northover to Glastonbury. A survey at the time of the Dissolution refers to 'running water' in the park. After this, when the area went out of use as a park and became meadows, it would still have carried some water until it silted up.

There are many water-courses, ditches, culverts and other cuttings in Glastonbury. The excavations around the Abbey precinct and in the former deer park at Wirral have hinted at their extent and complexity. Their purpose is, however, clear: to control the ubiquitous water flowing from springs, the sky, or the sea; to prevent flooding; to irrigate; to provide water, transport and power.

Resources, estates and boundaries

The power and wealth of a major abbey like Glastonbury depended on land-holdings, rather than on direct income centred on the abbey itself. The value of the holdings can be assessed by their extent in hectares, and by the resources they could provide, such as agricultural produce, honey, eels or grapes.

Not surprisingly, the estates of Glastonbury consisted of a heartland of local estates on fertile soils, within a day's reach (**84**); others in Somerset further away (see **77**); and

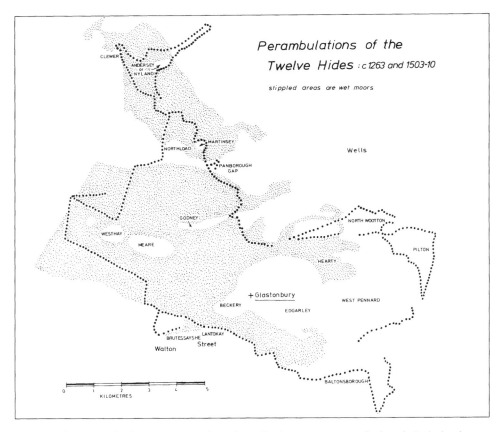

84 *The Abbey's heartland estates were mostly in the productive wet moor areas; the boundaries had to be periodically reasserted by formal perambulations.* After S.C. Morland, 1984

more in adjacent counties, especially in Dorset and Wiltshire. Land, and its resources, was acquired by royal charter or other legal means. The Abbey assiduously sought, from the late seventh century onwards, to increase its land, and repeatedly to confirm its title to them by fair means or foul: the latter included the forgery of charters (p.37). Even these forged charters are of value, however, in indicating what lands were being claimed at a particular time, and therefore their value to the Abbey.

The sources for our knowledge of the Abbey estates begin with charters of the late seventh century; the first complete survey of the Glastonbury estates is provided by the Domesday Book in the eleventh century; after the Conquest there are also royal confirmations, court records and surveys, and especially perambulations. These are the formal walking round the bounds of properties, from fixed point to fixed point, to affirm rights over the areas enclosed. Such points on the walk are often identifiable today from topographical clues or from the continuity of place-names. The last series of these walks was in the time of Abbot Bere, in 1503, 1507 and 1510 (see **84**).

The 'Twelve Hides' of Glastonbury have been much discussed. A hide was a unit of land, which notionally yielded resources sufficient for the sustenance of one household, but could vary considerably in actual size. The 'Twelve Hides' are often considered to be the heartland of the Abbey's possessions, dating back to its very early days, some would say to early Christian times, associated with the traditional number of hermits, each of whom is said to have dwelt in a cell around the nucleus of the Old Church (see **22**). More historically, the Twelve Hides constitute blocks of land, not all contiguous, which are referred to in written sources as 'a villa, a liberty, or a hundred, in which the Abbey enjoyed particular and valuable privileges'; these included exemption from certain taxation, and the rights to administer justice.

Study of the charters and other material shows how the land-holdings gradually increased from the eighth century onwards, laying the economic foundation for the importance of Glastonbury in the time of Dunstan, and for its medieval pre-eminence. From these can also be gathered the kinds of produce that would accrue to the Abbey (including that from arable land stored in the tithe barns discussed on p.133). There are the fruits, fuel and building material, from moor, pasture, meadow and woodland ('splendid and ample aldergroves, meadows and fruitful pastures' at Hearty); vineyards at Meare and Panborough; 7,000 eels from fisheries at Martinsey; and 'honey for the meadmaker' from Northload, with 30 salmon from the cellarer 'for the monks' feast'.

The perambulations not only indicate the boundaries of holdings, but also provide valuable clues about topography: which features of the modern landscape, and which names, can be traced back for hundreds of years. It is possible to retrace the steps of the party which set out on 26 July 1503, from Brutessayshe, where 3 ashes grew, and received the homage of Street:

> and proceeded . . . along the said ditch . . . direct to the Bridge of Wulgar with the beard . . . here bread, beer, wine and other victuals were

> provided at the Abbot's expense . . . then to where a cross once stood
> next to 4 oaks [Baltonsborough] . . . upstream to the house of the miller
> . . . and thus by Burybrigge to the Mere Stone that stands before the
> Abbot's door [Pilton] and there the first day's progress ended . . .

and so on, until the bounds had all been 'beaten'.

Much of the courses of the perambulations of about 1263 and those of 1503 to 1510 can be traced. The map (**84**) also shows how much of the heartland estates were wet moor, with the 'islands' which rise from them.

It is impossible now to reconstruct the names or extent of the twelve holdings themselves with any certainty but they included the local 'islands' (Beckery, Godney, Martinsey, Andersey, Westhay, Meare and Panborough). The principal named places are shown in **84**: the satellites of the Abbey.

At the daughter-houses of Andersey, Godney, Martinsey and Beckery, there were chapels (dedicated to St Andrew, the Holy Trinity, St Martin and St (?) Mary, respectively). Only the last, Beckery, has been excavated; it was shown to be a site of possibly early Anglo-Saxon origin (see below). At Martinsey (present-day Marchey Farm) there is an earthwork which could be the *vallum* (p.88) of an early monastic site. Field-walking here has located pre-Conquest pottery, and also much Roman material, confirming an early origin for the site as a whole.

Some medieval buildings survive on these heartland estates. At Pilton, the tithe barn has already been noted, and a fragment of the manor house may be medieval – a reputed summer palace of the abbots. It is at Meare, however, that most survives. The prehistoric settlement here has already been noted, on the side of a lake (Meare Pool), which had in medieval times a circumference of 8km (5 miles), drained only in the late eighteenth century. The church of St Mary (the same dedication as the Abbey) was in the abbots' care; much of it is fourteenth century, with a further work of Abbot Selwood in the later fifteenth century: his initials appear on the parapet of the south aisle. The Manor House was also a summer palace of the abbots, again principally fourteenth century. Close to this is the remarkable early fourteenth-century Fish House (**colour plate 25**). This was used both as a base for fishing in the Pool, and as a depot for the salting and storage of fish for the Abbey. The upper rooms provided living quarters, reached by an outer stairway.

One special machine utilised the resources of wind, water and animal power – the mill. The sluggish course of the River Brue or its tributaries was not conducive to the use of waterpower on a large scale, unless it could be ponded up in a mill-pond or other reservoir. There were, nevertheless, at least four watermills associated with the medieval Abbey (none is recorded before the Conquest or in Domesday Book). The possible evidence for a watermill close to the precinct at Chaingate has been noted above (p.123). Another at Street Bridge was in existence before 1163. The weir at Clyse Hole (see **82**) created a head of water for a millstream which powered the medieval mill at Beckery, and subsequently that at Northover (built about 1500), but this could only run when Beckery Mill was operating downstream.

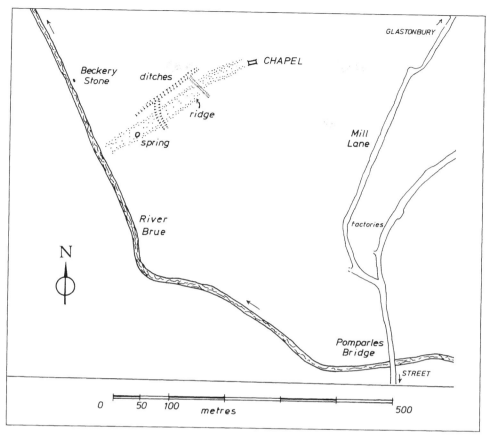

85 *The location of the monastery of Beckery, in low-lying land to the south-west of Glastonbury.*
After Rahtz and Hirst, 1974

There is no record of any of these watermills being used for fulling, or for any purpose other than the grinding of corn. This was probably also the sole function of windmills (invented only in the twelfth century). These are recorded at Glastonbury itself in 1244 and 1309, and at Street in 1255. A horse-mill is recorded in 1268.

Much of the analysis of these valuable sources has tended to be done in study and library. With some notable exceptions, there has been little fieldwork to amplify extensive details of the medieval and earlier landscapes. The more distant estates of the Abbey in Somerset in 1086 can be reconstructed from Domesday Book (see **77**).

Beckery

Beckery lies *c.*2km (over a mile) south-west of the Abbey, and is one of its 'daughter-houses'. Legends link the site with Irish connections, and in particular with St Bridget. Excavations have shown that it originated in Anglo-Saxon times as a small monastery with associated cemetery. A stone chapel, together with other structures, was built in the late Saxon period; this was enlarged and rebuilt in later centuries, surviving until the Dissolution.

Traditions from the twelfth century recount a visit to Beckery in 488 by the Irish St Bridget and how she left behind some of her possessions: a bag or wallet, a necklace, a small bell and some weaving implements, objects which were 'displayed and adored'. Later interpolations add that there was an oratory, dedicated to St Mary Magdalene; and, rather more fancifully, that King Arthur, resting at Glastonbury, was told by an angel in a dream to go to the hermitage on the 'island' of Beckery; he eventually went to the chapel, where the Virgin and the Infant Jesus appeared to him.

Written sources begin with a charter of dubious authenticity, purporting to date to 670, which gave Beckery to Abbot Berthwald. In a further (possibly genuine) charter of 971, a chapel is implied, and the site is named as 'Little Ireland'. Irish connections with Glastonbury do, in fact, go back to at least the ninth century; a *Life* of Dunstan (p.43) described how he was instructed by Irish teachers. The identification of Beckery as their abode is likely to be from a misinterpretation of the name as *Becc-Eriu*, in Irish meaning 'Little Ireland'; the name actually means 'Bee-keeper's island'.

Beckery is one of several such 'islands' in the area as noted above (p.146), outlying sites in the possession of the Abbey. Medieval references to Beckery include mention of 'repair' of the chapel in the late thirteenth century; and an interesting detail: 'the chapel in honour of . . . St Bridget, has a hole or opening in the southern part, and all who pass through it . . . will obtain forgiveness for all their sins'. This is reminiscent of the legends attached to holes in some prehistoric megaliths.

The site (**85**) is at the extreme westerly tip of the Glastonbury peninsula, an area just above the 7.6m (25ft) contour. Like the 'Mound' site (p.138), its low-lying location would render its lower areas liable to flooding; it would not, however, become a true island unless the waters rose to above 11m (36ft) above sea-level, a higher level than any recorded in geologically recent times. The summit of the potential island, on which the chapel complex lies, is at 12m (39ft), only just above the flood waters (**86**).

The whole area is dominated by the dramatic landmass of Wirral Hill. It would be the first place that a traveller to Glastonbury would reach by approaches from the west, by a water-route afforded by the River Brue (now canalised) (see **82**). Another attraction of the site was a spring. Associated with this was St Bride's Well. In the 1920s this was a shallow basin among brambles, marked by an inscribed stone. Unfortunately, the stone was later moved. It is now 100m (330ft) away, the original site is thus lost, but was presumably near the spring.

The ruins of the chapel were seen in the late eighteenth century, but had disappeared by the late nineteenth. The fields around, however, were still at that time called

'The Brides', preserving the memory of the tradition of St Bridget. John Morland, observing parchmarks, rediscovered the chapel in 1887. He skilfully excavated two buildings, the chapel complex and a priest's house. A more extensive excavation was carried out in 1967-8, for the Chalice Well Trust. As with every other site dug in Glastonbury, flints and Roman pottery indicate earlier frequentation.

The earlier Anglo-Saxon monastery

The earliest Anglo-Saxon buildings were of timber; most of the post-holes and timber-slots were for these, but some could be for grave shrines or grave-marker posts. The main group is interpreted as a chapel (**88**) orientated west-east. Inside this was a stone-lined grave (**colour plate 14**), clearly that of a person of exceptional importance, perhaps the original founder or hermit. The skeleton was of an adult male (25-35 years old) with arms extended and head turned to the south.

The presence of this grave here does not rule out the identification of the timber structure suggested above: but it is possible that this might have been a tomb-shrine, rather than a burial inside an oratory or chapel. Radiocarbon dating indicates that the skeleton could be as early as the sixth century or as late as the tenth.

The cemetery is of exceptional interest. It is the largest group of graves or skeletons to have been excavated in Glastonbury and the only one to have been

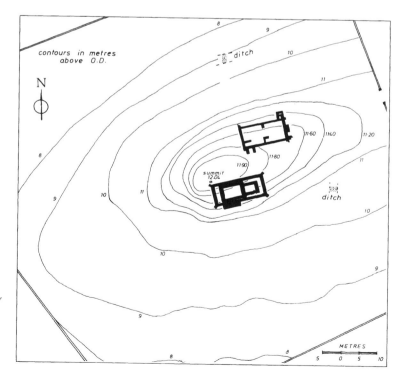

86 *Beckery, like Glastonbury itself, is a peninsula rather than an 'island', with the monastery built on its highest part*

87 *Graves in the cemetery, dug to different depths; view from the east*

examined by modern specialists. Bones of 63 individuals were found. It is likely that the total number did not exceed 100.

The graves are to some extent in rows, with heads lined up north-south; this implies the use of wooden grave-markers. The orientation of the skeletons, notionally west-east, averaged well south of west, at 258° (range 234 to 275°); that of the chapels is similar, at 259 to 260°, implying some continuity. It will be seen, however (**88**), that a group in the north-east area are slightly radial, the heads pointing more towards the nuclear grave in the chapel. Most of the skeletons were fully extended with arms straight down the sides. An unusual feature (in a Christian context) is that six skeletons were face downwards. This prone position is associated in pagan contexts with evil-doers such as witches or criminals. In this community there must have been some reason for the special treatment; perhaps they had committed some mortal sin, or were experiencing some form of penance.

All but three were adult males – a very clear indication that this was a male monastic community. The exceptions were one female and two children (6-7 and 8-9 years old). The children may have been novitiates or orphaned relatives of a monk. One was buried close to the female, and may have been her child. She could have been a servant; or at the other social extreme, a patron who wished to be buried there; or a traveller who fell ill and died nearby. The only other features of interest are common to all Glastonbury sites except the Tor drainage ditches – vital in these moorside edges. Since it seems likely that Beckery, like other daughter-houses, was founded by the established Abbey, a date for the earliest monastery in the eighth or ninth century seems probable; though of some duration, to judge by the size of the cemetery.

The community may have begun as the abode of a hermit (possibly the occupant of the nuclear grave), whose reputation attracted others to join him (as on the Tor?). If the graves are spread over two or three centuries, there may never have been more than a dozen monks at one time, but the number may have been greater if the life of the cemetery was shorter.

Little can be said about the life-style of the monastic community. Finds were few; animal bones suggest that cattle, sheep, pigs and poultry contributed to the diet, together with edible shell-fish. Sheep and goats may have been kept also for wool and dairy products; and there were also bones of a dog.

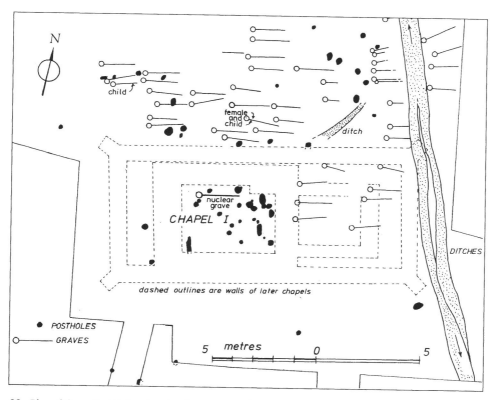

88 *Plan of the earliest timber chapel and cemetery, Beckery; note the west-east orientation of the graves set out in rows. After Rahtz and Hirst, 1974*

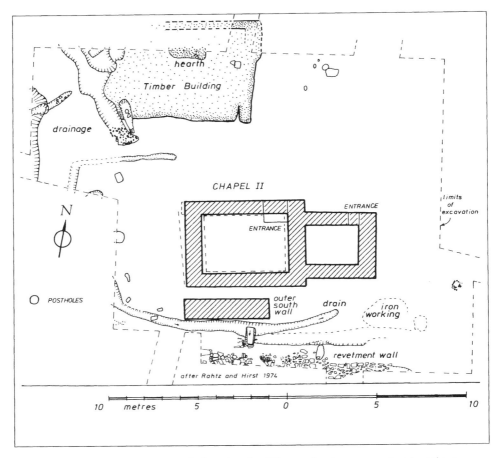

89 *The late Anglo-Saxon monastery, Beckery (see also **92**); note that there were no burials at this time*

The later Anglo-Saxon monastery (colour plate 15)

The monastic complex was radically changed in the late Anglo-Saxon period, in the late tenth or eleventh century. A new chapel, built in stone, replaced the earlier timber structure; the cemetery went out of use, and a wooden building, drains and other features were added (**89**).

The new chapel (**90**) was 10m (33ft) long overall. Its nave enclosed the site of the earlier chapel or tomb-shrine with the nuclear grave. The walls were of stone, four courses surviving in place; they were rendered in stucco. The roof was of thatch, turf, or (as in **92**) wooden shingles. There were two entrances, one at the north-east corner of the nave, the other at the north-east corner of the chancel. Northerly doorways are unusual; here, however, there were two constraints. The first was that the chapel should perpetuate the location of the earlier nucleus; and secondly the ground was firmer and more level to the north; and this is where other buildings were located.

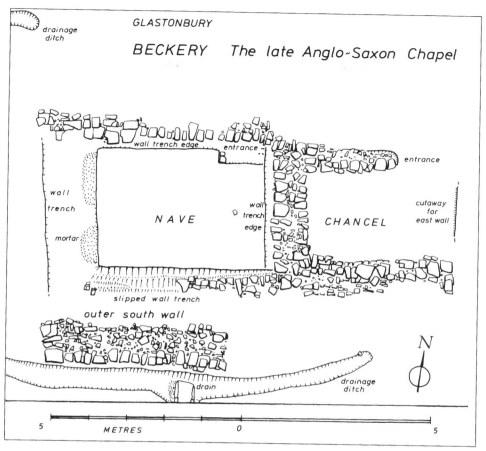

90 *Plan of the late Anglo-Saxon chapel, Beckery; note the outer wall; the east and west ends have been removed to reuse their stone.* After Rahtz and Hirst, 1974

A strange feature is the outer south wall, parallel to the south wall of the nave, with a metre-wide gap between. One possible explanation is that it may have carried a staircase to a gallery over the west end of the nave, where perhaps relics were kept or shown (possibly those said to have been left by St Bridget?). Alternatively there may have been some structure here which contained the 'hole in the southern part of the chapel, through which all who passed would receive forgiveness of their sins'.

The chapel continued in use after the Norman Conquest, into the thirteenth century. In a life of over two centuries there was not surprisingly some rebuilding. The nave entrance was rebuilt with a Norman chevron-decorated arch in the twelfth century. One voussoir (arch-stone) of this found in the rubble allowed the reconstruction of the arch shown in **91**; its internal diameter of 1.2m (4ft) fits precisely into the entrance gap shown in **90**. Around the chapel were drainage ditches and iron-working hearths and, to the north, a timber building measuring *c.*8 by 6m (26 by 20ft) (**89 & 92**).

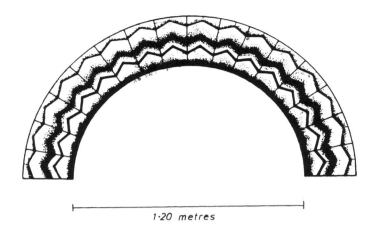

1·20 metres

91 *Reconstruction of twelfth-century arch of the north doorway of the late Anglo-Saxon chapel; this is based on a single voussoir found (one of the arch-stones)*

The occupation of the site during these centuries may have comprised no more than a chapel, and a house for its resident priest (see **92** & **93**). There is no evidence of any graves, or of communal life. The structures served, however, to perpetuate the memory of the earlier monastic community. It may be imagined that by the tenth century the traditions of St Bridget and the Irish connection were being exploited, enough to secure a steady interest in the site by pilgrims to the now famous Glastonbury area. Some of the bronze finds suggest that the little stone chapel may have had some quite exotic fittings or portable objects, such as little boxes or reliquaries.

The medieval chapel and priest's house (colour plate 15)

The latest chapel at Beckery was of conventional medieval plan, a rectangle with diagonal buttresses, *c.*15m (50ft) long (**93**). The earlier chapel lay wholly within this rectangle; it is likely, as often happens, that the older chapel was left standing until the new chapel was built around it.

It seems probable that this was the work done in the late thirteenth century, the ruin of which survived to the eighteenth century. The chapel was substantially built, with deep foundations; the roof was of possibly Cornish slates, and there was a tiled floor. Some of the decorated floor tiles can be dated to *c.*1250-90. The only entrance located was in the centre of the north wall of the nave.

Other buildings lay to the north, including the 'priest's house'; but only its south edge was uncovered in the recent excavations. Outside the southern porch there was a substantial fence, which separated the chapel from the more secular area of the other buildings. The 1887 plan shows also internal divisions, a hearth or chimney stack, and a lavatory block (*garde-robe*) at the north-east corner.

92 *Reconstruction drawing of the later Anglo-Saxon monastery – the practical aspects of monastic life are well illustrated.* Judith Dobie

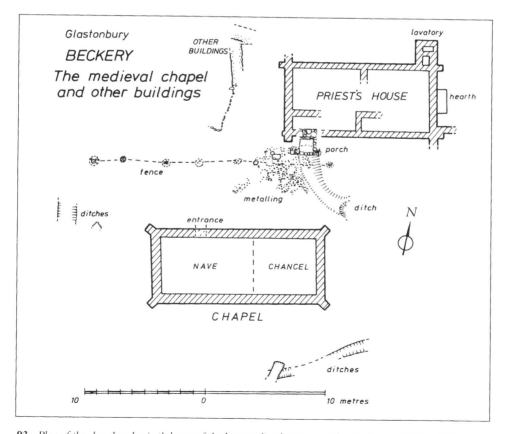

93 *Plan of the chapel and priest's house of the later medieval centuries.* After Rahtz and Hirst, 1974

The chapel and other buildings represent an expansion of the provisions for pilgrims in the high Middle Ages, both for worship and perhaps also accommodation; the scale of the priest's house may be compared with the final buildings on the Tor.

10

GLASTONBURY IN MODERN TIMES

The Abbey

The role of the Church of England in preserving what was left of the Abbey was described in chapter 7; the principal damage since then has been done by archaeologists.

The Church has, however, also been active in reviving spiritual aspects of the Abbey, which remains a great monument to the Christian faith. A pilgrimage is still held, and services are celebrated in the shell of the church which 15,000 people attend. There are impressive processions of clerics from many parishes, in their finery; and recitals, lectures and retreats. It is possible to buy a range of souvenirs – pilgrimage badges, Dunstan badges, car stickers and tea towels: it is (mildly) reminiscent of Lourdes.

The Roman Catholic Church also holds its own celebration (though not in the Abbey); but attempts are being made towards ecumenical integration. A major appeal was launched to build a new visitor centre in the Abbey, the principal signatories of which were the Archbishop of Canterbury and the (Roman Catholic) Bishop of Clifton. This work involved some archaeological excavation (costed at £20,000) in advance of the building work. Apart from these special occasions, the ruins attract many visitors, some 150,000 in recent years.

The town after the Dissolution

Glastonbury, as a town, declined with the demise of the Abbey as a functioning institution. It may be envisaged in the following centuries as a place that had rather lost its identity and fallen on bad times, around the increasingly derelict ruins – in contrast to nearby Wells, remaining elegant around its surviving cathedral.

It survived, however, as a local market centre, and there remained the need to cater for antiquarian visitors. It was perhaps the relative lack of expansion that fortunately limited encroachment on the precinct, except on the eastern side of Magdalene Street. Although the ordinary medieval town buildings have mostly been replaced, the tenements remain, the long narrow gardens typical of medieval burgage plots.

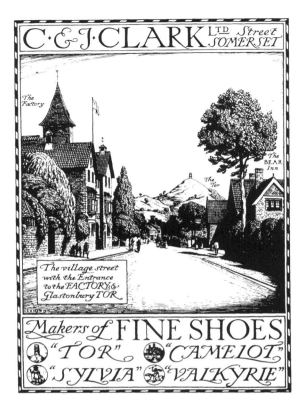

94 *Advertisement for Clark's shoes in the early twentieth century; this illustrates a romantic and conservationist approach to commerce*

The streets still afford a fine townscape of notable buildings of the eighteenth and nineteenth centuries, among them the Pump Rooms (1754), built during a brief spa revival (below), and the Town Hall in Magdalene Street (1818) (degraded to a cinema in the post-war decades). The medieval market cross (demolished in 1808) was replaced in 1848 by a rather fine monument recalling in its style the Eleanor crosses of eastern England. The highway area around the market cross was improved and repaved in 1995, moving the vehicles away from this important historic structure.

Major attempts at extending the commercial importance of Glastonbury began with the construction of the Glastonbury canal in 1834, 20km (12 miles) long, from Glastonbury to the River Parrett at Highbridge. This was 2m (over 6ft) deep and thus able to take shallow draught vessels. There was extensive traffic on this waterway to Gloucester, Bristol, Newport and Cardiff; goods moved included timber, iron, salt, coal and slate. The canal survived for only 20 years before it was replaced by the Somerset and Dorset railway branch line to Highbridge.

All attempts at making Glastonbury a successful town have rather neglected the preservation of its historic past. This has led among other things to the unattractive approach to the Abbey described in chapter 7; and, recently, to the destruction of the open ground of Wirral Park to the west of the town by supermarkets.

In 1994 a bypass was constructed on the west side of the town and this road has transformed Glastonbury by taking most of the traffic from the centre and providing access for housing and commercial development on the western approaches to the town.

There has, however, been one major exception: that is the development of the footwear and sheepskin industries by Clarks and Morlands. Both families are Quakers and have promoted industry for the benefit of the community. Development has been sensitive and paternalistic, as were the developments elsewhere by the other great Quaker giants of Fry, Rowntree and Cadbury. The Clark factory in Street is in neo-Tudor style (**94**), and the shoes in this advertisement are named after the Tor, Arthurian Camelot, the Nordic Valkyrie, and a shepherdess named Sylvia: utilizing romantic associations to good effect.

The former Morland and Bailey sheepskin factories on the western edge of the town have been a sign of dereliction and decay in recent years. These sites are about to be 'regenerated' and there will be opportunities for investigating the early medieval water systems, mills and associated structures. Some of these industrial buildings make a valuable contribution to the landscape and character of Glastonbury's working heritage and provide an historic landmark in the sea of new houses and modern sheds.

The Spa and Chalice Well theatre

The role of the great spring of Chalice Well in laying the foundations for the fame of Glastonbury has been discussed in chapter 2, and its use for the Abbey in chapter 8. The water again attracted attention in the eighteenth century. One Matthew Chancellor had a dream, in which he was cured of asthma by drinking the waters of a clear stream at Glastonbury on seven successive Sunday mornings; and this came true. Word spread, and in 1751, 10,000 people flocked to be cured. A header tank of brick was built underground, adjacent to the medieval well-house (see **78**); this can still be entered when the well is drained. Water was led down the valley and under Magdalene Street into a pump-house. A list of diseases cured includes 'King's evil', blindness, ulcers and deafness. The 'spa' was short-lived, but people continue to drink and bathe in the water, and claim cures. A recent distinguished 'patient' was Prince Charles, after he broke his arm in 1990.

The property belonged, at the end of the last century, to a Roman Catholic order, and it was presumably they who gave it the name of Chalice Well, in pursuance of the Arthur/Grail myth. The story that Joseph of Arimathea came to Glastonbury and was buried there with two silver cruets filled with the blood and sweat of Jesus originated in the mid-thirteenth century in an interpolation to William of Malmesbury (p.59). The belief that Joseph washed these vessels in the spring, and that the first Christians were baptised there, are recent accretions. Earlier in this century, the property passed into the hands of Alice Buckton (author

95 *The fountain at Chalice Well, showing the concretion building up from the iron-rich water of the spring*

of *Eager Heart*), who built an open-air theatre in the valley above the well, of which the foundation platform still survives. Here was established in 1912 a remarkable event – the Glastonbury Festival (not to be confused with the modern one described below). The idea was to establish nothing less than an English Bayreuth, a National Festival Theatre for Music, Mystic Drama and the Arts. Rutland Boughton (1878-1960) was the founder. The idea was discouraged by George Bernard Shaw. In a letter to Boughton he castigated him:

I greatly mistrust your project of a series of Arthurian music dramas. You will simply provide a second-hand Ring. The Ring itself would never have existed if it had not been to Wagner an expression of his strongest religious and social beliefs . . . you might do better . . . (as do Strauss and Elgar) with the modern world in a crisp and powerful style, making a clean sweep of the tremolandos and the sentimental and grandiose modulations of the nineteenth century.

Boughton's famous opera, *The Immortal Hour*, was nevertheless given its first performance at Glastonbury on 26 August 1914 – a work 'suffused with that ethereal otherworld atmosphere which is the essence of the Celtic spirit'. The best-known aria recalls the legends of the Tor, rising above Chalice Well:

How beautiful they are, the lordly ones,
Who dwell in the hill, the hollow hill.
They laugh, and are glad, and are terrible.

The work went on to play to packed houses in London in the 1920s.

Plans for elaborate choral dramas, including Wagner and episodes from the Arthurian cycle, were aborted because of the 1914-18 war. They resumed in later years, however; again Shaw writes (1932):

What you have to rub in is that opera is impossible in any complete artistic sense under commercial conditions . . . when we have Comm-unism and plenty of leisure, with money enough to provide our own houses and costumes . . . we shall just begin to make *opera live*.

Shaw himself lectured to the Glastonbury Festival. In 1959 the property was vested in the Chalice Well Trust, who have developed the valley into a pilgrim centre. They have made splendid gardens, basins and fountains with the water, encrusted red with iron (**95**).

Archaeology and the historic environment

It was the Trust who sponsored the excavations at Chalice Well, the Tor and Beckery. The circumstances of the Abbey excavations in 1904-78 have been discussed above in chapter 7, and the 'Lake Village' work of Bulleid and Gray in chapter 3.

It should be stressed that all these were research excavations, carried out solely to acquire knowledge, and (in the case of the Abbey) to help in presenting the site to the public. All more recent work has been in response to threats from commer-cial or other development and has taken place under the auspices of English

Heritage. There have been excavations in the town in Silver Street, and other places on the edge of the Abbey precinct; St John's Church; Wirral Park (the canal and other features); and the Mound. These have been done, mostly in archaeologically difficult conditions, by members of the University of Birmingham Unit; by Jane Carr; and by the 'resident archaeologists', Nancy and Charles Hollinrake, whose work has figured several times in this book.

The largest ongoing project has, however, been the work in the Somerset Levels, in advance of commercial peat extraction. John and Bryony Coles were also supported here by English Heritage, and their own Universities of Cambridge and Exeter. A major problem was that having so skilfully demonstrated the existence of Neolithic and later waterlogged trackways and settlements, they had to cope with the dehydration of the peat brought about by the lowering of the water table in the process of peat removal. Special measures are being taken in a few places to reflood areas (which will also safeguard wildlife), but most of the buried wooden structures will disappear within a decade or two, to the great loss of archaeology. Responsibility for the work of the Somerset Levels Project was passed to Somerset County Council in 1989 and a number of projects have been carried out in the Glastonbury area recently. The Environment Agency recently commissioned a review of archaeological sites preserved in peat. One of the main objectives was to see what were the likely effects of peat desiccation on many of the important archaeological sites such as Glastonbury or Meare Lake Villages. The report concluded that all the known archaeological sites preserved in the peat around Glastonbury were at a significant risk from the effects of peat drying out and wasting away.

The need for archaeology is now a recognised requirement as part of the planning system and both the county and district councils ensure that appropriate archaeological research and recording is done in advance of development in and around the town.

No mention of the archaeology of Glastonbury would be complete without reference to the Glastonbury Antiquarian Society. This was formed in 1886 with Arthur Bulleid as its first President. A museum was established under the Town Hall. In 1892, the 'Lake Village' excavations began, and the Society became responsible for a site of international importance. They own the field in which the Glastonbury village lay. The finds from this site were later transferred to the Tribunal. The Society has also been active in publication, including two volumes on the Glastonbury Lake Village, Arthur Bulleid's *The Lake Villages of Somerset* (now in its seventh edition) and a monograph on the excavations at Beckery.

The Glastonbury Fair and the alternative society

Fairs were frequently held in medieval times in the vicinity of churches, and it was doubtless the numerous visitors to the Abbey and town which gave rise to the fairs held in Fairfield, the former Wirral Park. Metal-detectors working there have found thousands of coins dating from the mid-eighteenth century onwards, together with buttons, keys and toys. Such evidence of secular activity may be contrasted with that from the neighbouring Convent Field, the scene of large Roman Catholic gatherings in the 1930s, associated with pilgrimages. Detectors here have found five crucifixes, ten religious medallions and nine thimbles. The latter were lost when the nuns gave sewing lessons on this spot.

After 1971, the fair (now Fayre) took on a rather different complexion, at various venues near the town, at Pilton. It is now a major pop festival, attended by many tens of thousands of young campers in tents and tepees, of all 'alternative' persuasions. There have, as seems inseparable from such events, been problems of rubbish disposal, nudity and drug traffickers; drug officers were rather perturbed to find that the symptoms of LSD poisoning were very similar to those caused by a heavy intake of Somerset cider! But on the whole, the occasion is one of great enjoyment; the venue has a special attraction because of the association of Glastonbury with everything irrational discussed earlier – the Zodiac, the Maze, Arthur, the Grail and Joseph; to which are now added ley-lines, UFOs and corn-circles. The impact of the modern festival on the local landscape, community and economy is considerable and the modern 'pilgrimage' to the Glastonbury festival provides an eclectic experience for all ages.

The Fayre is, however, only a particular manifestation of a much wider phenomenon, the attraction in the 1960s and 1970s of Glastonbury to old and young people from all over the world, described in the Guardian (20.12.69) as 'hippies, poets, mystics, and weirdies'. They are drawn by what are known as 'vibes', vibrations emanating from Glastonbury's long myth and history, 'a modern Mecca for the Age of Aquarius'. The 'Love People', not surprisingly, antagonised the more sober citizens of Glastonbury. 'Half the town accused them of being unwashed, the others (notably the Trustees of Chalice Well) of using the waters for communal ablutions, shaving and washing of jeans'. Glastonbury was the 'centre of cosmic power in . . . Atlantean days . . . there is an increasing influx of Atlantean souls on this planet, feeling foreign in a strange world'. Glastonbury is also the real Jerusalem (Bristol is Sodom!).

Some echoes of this still continue. A proliferation of shops has sprung up, selling very odd objects and especially an astonishing variety of books (and this includes the Abbey bookstall). One shop, alongside a notice ARMS ARE FOR HUGGING, advertises books on, among other things, Love and Happiness, Astrology, Crystals, Earth Mysteries and Sacred Sites, and Personal Growth. A special nucleus, The Glastonbury Experience, has signposts to shops and studios sited within a courtyard, directing visitors to Miracles, Pendragon, Apothecary, Star Child, Wholefoods, The Spirit of the Celt and the Gaia Healing Wing: ecumenical indeed!

Whose Glastonbury is it?

This question echoes that applied to another famous place – Stonehenge. Ley-liners claim that this is linked to Glastonbury by a ley-line 50km (31 miles) long, on the axis of the Abbey. It is said that UFO sightings are especially numerous around Warminster, about half-way between the two places.

Who owns Stonehenge? (Chippindale 1990) was a compilation arising from a session at the *World Archaeological Conference* at Southampton in 1986. Contributors included a ley-liner, who is also director of the Centre for Earth Mysteries Studies; the secular Arch-Druid; and an archaeological 'establishment man'. A similar compendium could arise from very similar problems and competing interests at Glastonbury. Many of these have been mentioned in this book: the struggle of the rational against the draw of the irrational; pilgrimages for Christians and those of a more secular if mystic character; 'ordinary, decent townspeople' who want to live in a quiet world unworried by drug abuse, armed beggars and violence; academics and conservationists who want a quiet, historic, preserved Glastonbury, rather than a modernised town cluttered by tourists, cars, unnecessary shops and supermarkets; archaeologists witnessing the buried heritage being destroyed by developments sponsored by building and peat-extracting giants. The environment is threatened in many ways.

These are problems that are universal in the modern world, in which the claims of competing interests are struggled for, it is to be hoped without direct conflict; but nowhere are the results so diverse and tragic as at Glastonbury.

WHERE TO VISIT

In *Glastonbury* itself, it will be evident from the text which places are worth visiting or studying.

The **Abbey**, with its convenient carpark, should be the starting point, armed with one of the numerous guidebooks on sale in the Abbey bookshop; the ruins and laid-out foundations are worth extensive study, as is the visitor centre.

Also in the town centre is the **Tribunal** with its excellent museum display (English Heritage); **St John's Church**; **St Benignus'** (now Benedict's) **Church**; the **Hospital of St Mary Magdalene** (off Magdalene Street); and the **'Jacoby' Chapel** in Bove Town. This would probably be a good point to repair to the **George and Pilgrim Inn**, a fine medieval building, which still provides food and drink.

To the west, but still within walking distance, are **Chalice Well**, the **Somerset Rural Life Museum** (Somerset County Council) which incorporates the **Abbey Barn**; throughout the summer there are numerous craft demonstrations, ranging from basket-making to pole lathe 'bodging'; and many special events, exhibitions and farming activities. From here one walks up to **Chalice Well** (a pleasant haven from the bustle of the town); and thence up to the **Tor** (National Trust). This is a stiff climb, but a magnificent view awaits the walker on the summit. Chapter 6 should be read before this visit; only the tower of **St Michael's Church** survives of the buildings described; but one can see where they lie buried, and weigh the pros and cons about the terraces which surround the Tor hill.

A short cycle or car drive (or a longish walk) towards Street will take the traveller to **Wirral Hill** (note the traces of the canal on the south-east side of the road) and to **Pomparles Bridge**.

If you are adventurous, a walk will lead to **Beckery**; nothing of the buildings described in chapter 9 is now visible, but the site is worth visiting to see its topography. The former Morland's and Bailey's Sheepskin works dominate this side of town and most of the site is undergoing demolition prior to its 'regeneration' as an employment area and potential heritage park.

On the Meare road the bumps of the **Glastonbury 'Lake Village'** can still be seen (chapter 3), and the village of **Meare**, with its **church**, **manor house** and the **Fish House**. Between Shapwick and Westhay is a small but informative display at the Peat Moors Visitor Centre illustrating the work of the Somerset

Levels Project (John and Bryony Coles). This was opened in 1992 to celebrate the centenary of Bulleid's discovery. Two Iron Age roundhouses modelled on buildings from Glastonbury Lake village (**colour plate 4**) were built in 1992 to celebrate the centenary of Bulleid's discovery. The centre has several reconstructed prehistoric track ways, an Iron Age style log boat and small displays covering the story of archaeology, nature conservation and the history of peat digging. This centre is open to visitors from March until October with a varied programme of events and demonstrations of ancient crafts and technologies. It also provides a useful base for visiting the nearby National Nature Reserve at Shapwick Heath. Refreshments and other facilities are also available at the centre.

Really dedicated walkers can try to follow the perambulations of the '**Twelve Hides**' described in chapter 9; to do this they should be provided with large scale maps (the 1:25,000 scale O.S. map is suitable) and a copy of Stephen Morland's excellent paper (1984).

A drive towards Shepton Mallet will lead through **Ponter's Ball** (chapter 3); it is well worth walking the whole length of this (with due permission and deference to farmers' interests).

Finally, a visit to **Taunton** is necessary, to see the excellent county museum in the Castle (Somerset County Council). This exhibits material of all periods from the area around Glastonbury, and especially the remarkable finds from the 'Lake Villages'.

Modern Glastonbury (chapter 10) with its industrial development and tourist attractions will be all too evident in the town; but the surrounding countryside is still relatively unspoilt, and one of the best areas in the West Country for an extended visit or holiday.

FURTHER READING

BIBLIOGRAPHY

GLOSSARY

INDEX

FURTHER READING

2 Why Glastonbury? Environment and resources

Dale and Gannaway (1960) give a good account of the geology, and a useful survey of the whole region of Glastonbury and Street. For the debate on changes in sea/land levels and marine transgression, see Hawkins (1973), and Heyworth and Kidson (1982). The rivers and seawalls are discussed by Kelting (1968); and Williams (1970) is the classic work on the drainage of the Levels. Resources of the area are principally discussed by prehistorians (e.g. Coles and Orme 1980), though there is also much on this in Williams (1970).

3 Prehistoric and Roman settlement

A good general guide for the reader to the archaeology of Somerset is Aston and Burrow (1982, re-published in 1991), which has an extensive bibliography. The environment of the 'Lake Villages' is considered by Houseley (1988), Coles and Orme (1980), and of wetlands in general by Coles and Coles (1989). The work of Coles and Orme (later Coles and Coles) is described in detail in a series of publications, the Somerset Levels Papers. The Sweet Track is fully published (Coles and Coles 1986); the dendrochronological dating (tree-ring) is in Hillam *et al.* 1990. The classic study of the 'Lake Villages' themselves is that of Bulleid (fifth ed. 1958). This is the traditional description, but a remarkable modern theoretical analysis (used for **12**) is that by Clarke (1972). For Bulleid himself, see Coles, Goodall and Minnitt (1992). For Roman temples and their survival see Rahtz and Watts (1979) and for Pagans Hill in particular Rahtz and Watts (1991). The Cannington cemetery is now published (Rahtz, Hirst and Wright, 2000).

The extent of Roman Christianity in Britain is discussed by Thomas (1981). The Pagan/Christian transition in the west is considered by Rahtz (1991); and more widely by Watts (1991, 1998) and Woodward (1992). For a detailed discussion on the extent of Roman Christianity in Somerset see Leach (2002); for a discussion on the late Roman amulet from Shepton Mallet see Leach (2001).

4 History

Costen (1992) is a very readable general account of the origins of Somerset before medieval times. The Dark Ages in Somerset are discussed by Rahtz and Fowler (1972), and Rahtz (1982). Dumville

(1977 and 1990) is the best critical reading for the difficult texts of pre-Anglo-Saxon times. Early Christianity is, of course, the subject of numerous books and papers, but in general Thomas (1971) and Morris (1989) are recommended; and (for Somerset) Radford (1962), Dunning (1976), and Aston and Burrow (1982/1991); also see Harris (2003).

A good general guide to the geography of Anglo-Saxon England is provided by Hill (1981), and to the archaeology by Wilson (ed.) (1976). The most accessible modern history of the Abbey is by Carley (1988); this is a useful complement to the present book, as it deals in detail especially with written sources, and with people. The text of William of Malmesbury is available in Latin and in translation in Scott (1981). Special topics have recently been explored in Abrams and Carley (eds) (1991). The earlier works of Robinson (1921, 1923 a and b, 1926, 1927, and 1953-4) are still well worth reading.

5 Myth and legend

The background to the history and archaeology of 'Arthur' is provided by Alcock (1971) and Morris (1973); the associated (including Glastonbury) are described in Ashe (ed.) (1968) and Radford and Swanton (1975). For the nature of British mythology see Ashe (1990). The badges worn by pilgrims are fully listed, and the Glastonbury examples illustrated by Mitchener (1986). The Glastonbury legends and tradition are generously interpreted by Carley (1988) and critically by Gransden (1976). The Zodiac is sympathetically reviewed by Burrow (1983), with references to the works of Katherine Maltwood.

6 Glastonbury Tor

The full publication of the excavations is by Rahtz (1971) with a reconsideration in Rahtz and Watts (1991). For the background to mazes, see Fisher and Gerster (1992).

For a recent review and interpretation of Glastonbury Tor and the story of mazes see Rahtz (2002).

7 The Abbey and its precinct

A recent and readable survey of English religious houses, to put Glastonbury in perspective, is in this series, by Coppack (1990). Willis (1866) is still the best source for the architecture of the Abbey, though a more popular account will be found in Pevsner (1958). The reports on the excavations in the earlier part of the century are scattered in the *Proceedings of the Somerset Archaeological and Natural History Society* (later *Somerset Archaeology and Natural History*), *Somerset and Dorset Notes and Queries*, and *Antiquity*. A summary is by Radford (1981).

For Bligh Bond, see Bond (1918) on his methods, and Kenawell (1965) for his biography (which also has his excavation reports). The brass plate was reconsidered by Goodall (1986). The seal was first discussed by Watkin (1948-9). The details of the garden are from Keil (1959-60).

The impact of Glastonbury Abbey in Somerset is by Dunning in his book on Somerset monasteries (2001).

8 Town and environs

The best handbook to take on a perambulation of the town is still Pevsner (1958). The town is also the subject of a paper by Aston and Leech (1977). The Tribunal is reconsidered in a paper by Dunning (1991). The Somerset barns are described by Bond and Weller (1991). The full report on Chalice Well is by Rahtz (1964). The best short History and Guide is by Dunning (1994) which includes walking tours of the town and the abbey.

9 Beyond Glastonbury: routes by land and water, estates, wealth and satellites

The material on routes is largely from publications that are in preparation or in the press, or still in ms form, kindly made available by Stephen Morland.

For the estates see Morland (1970, 1984 and 1986), the latter with details of the perambulation of the Twelve Hides. Beckery is fully published in Rahtz and Hirst (1974).

For a discussion on the Anglo-Saxon canal at Glastonbury see the Hollinrakes (1992).

10 Glastonbury in modern times

The visitor to the town and Abbey will find numerous publications on sale on current trends; the reader of this book will have been suitably forewarned.

BIBLIOGRAPHY

Abrams, L. and Carley, J.P. (eds.) (1991), *The Archaeology and History of Glastonbury Abbey*, Boydell Press, Woodbridge.

Abrams, L. (1993), 'Saint Patrick and Glastonbury Abbey', in Dumville, D.N. (1993), *Saint Patrick, AD 493-1993*, Boydell Press, Woodbridge, 233-244.

Abrams, L. (1996), *Anglo-Saxon Glastonbury: church and endowment*, Boydell Press, Woodbridge.

Alcock, L. (1971), *Arthur's Britain*, Penguin, London.

Ashe, G. (1968), *The Quest for Arthur's Britain*, Pall Mall Press, London.

Ashe, G. (1990), *Mythology of the British Isles*, Methuen, London.

Aston, M. and Burrow, I. (eds.) (1982/1991), *The Archaeology of Somerset*, Somerset County Council, Taunton (reprinted 1991).

Aston, M. and Leech, R. (1977), 'Glastonbury', in M. Aston and R. Leech (eds.), *Historic Towns in Somerset*, Committee for Rescue Archaeology in Avon, Gloucestershire and Somerset, Gloucester, 57-65.

Blackman, D.J. (ed.) (1973), *Marine Archaeology, Proceedings of the 23rd Symposium Colston Research Society*, London.

Bond, C.J. and Weller, J.B. (1991), 'The Somerset Barns of Glastonbury Abbey', in Abrams and Carley (eds.) (1991), 57-87.

Bond, F.B. (1918), *The Gate of Remembrance*, Blackwell, Oxford.

Brunning, R. *et al.* (1996), 'Excavations at Benedict Street, Glastonbury, 1993', *Somerset Archaeology and Natural History* 139, 17-45.

Bulleid, A. (1958), *The Lake Villages of Somerset* (fifth edition), Glastonbury Antiquarian Society, Glastonbury.

Burrow, I. (1983), 'Star-spangled Avalon', *Popular Archaeology*, 4.8, 28-31.

Carley, J. (1985), *The Chronicle of Glastonbury Abbey*, Boydell Press, Woodbridge.

Carley, J. (1988), *Glastonbury Abbey and The Holy House of the Moors Adventurous*, Boydell Press, Woodbridge.

Carley, J. (1994), 'More pre-Conquest manuscripts from Glastonbury Abbey', *Anglo-Saxon England* 23, 265-281.

Carley, J. (ed.) (2000), *Glastonbury Abbey and the Arthurian tradition*, D.S. Brewer, Woodbridge.

Carver, M. (ed.) (1993), *In Search of Cult*, Boydell Press, Woodbridge.

Chippindale, C. (ed.) (1990), *Who Owns Stonehenge?*, Batsford, London.

Clarke, D.L. (1972), 'A provisional model of an Iron Age society and its settlement system', in Clarke, D.L. (ed.) (1972), *Models in Archaeology*, Methuen, London, 801-69.

Coles J. and Orme, B. (1980), *Prehistory of the Somerset Levels*, Somerset Levels Project, Cambridge.

Coles, B. and Coles, J. (1986), *Sweet Track to Glastonbury*, Thames and Hudson, London.

Coles, B. and Coles, J. (1989), *People of the Wetlands: Bogs, Bodies, and Lake-Dwellers*, Thames and Hudson, London.

Coles, J., Goodall, A. and Minnitt, S. (1992), *Arthur Bulleid and the Glastonbury Lake Villages*, Somerset Levels Project and Somerset County Council, Taunton.

Coles, J. & Minnitt, S. (1995), *'Industrious and fairly civilized': the Glastonbury Lake Village*, Somerset Levels Project, [Thorverton].

Coppack, G. (1990), *Abbeys and Priories*, Batsford/English Heritage, London.

Costen, M. (1992), *The Origins of Somerset*, Manchester University Press, Manchester.

Dale, R.W. and Gannaway, LT. (1960), *Report of Survey relating to Glastonbury and Street area*, Somerset County Council, Taunton.

Dodwell, C.R (1982), *Anglo-Saxon Art: A New Perspective*, Manchester University Press.

Dumville, D. (1977), 'Sub-Roman Britain: History and Legend', *History* 62.205, 173-92.

Dumville, D. (1990), *Histories and Pseudo-histories of the Insular Middle Ages*, Variorum, Oxford.

Dunning, R.W. (1976), *Christianity in Somerset*, Somerset County Council, Taunton.

Dunning, R.W. (1991), 'The Tribunal, Glastonbury, Somerset', in Abrams and Carley (eds.) (1991), 89-93.

Dunning, R.W. (1994), *Glastonbury: history and guide*, Alan Sutton, Stroud.

Dunning R.W. (2001) *Somerset Monasteries,* Tempus, Stroud.

Finberg, H.P.R. (1967), 'St Patrick at Glastonbury', *Irish Ecclesiastical Record* 107.6, 345-61.

Fisher, A. and Gerster, G. (1992), *The Art of the Maze*, Weidenfeld and Nicolson, London.

Fowler, P.J. (ed.) (1972), *Archaeology and the Landscape*, John Baker, London.

Gathercole C. 1996 *Glastonbury An extensive urban survey.* Somerset County Council and English Heritage. A version of this report will be available on the SCC Heritage web site.

Gerald of Wales (1980 ed.), *The Journey through Wales and the Description of Wales*, Penguin, Harmondsworth.

Gilpin, W. (1798), *Observations on the Western Parts of England*, London.

Goodall, J.A. (1986), 'The Glastonbury Abbey Memorial Plate reconsidered', *Antiquaries Journal* 66, 364-7.

Gransden, A. (1976), 'The growth of the Glastonbury traditions and legends in the twelfth century', *Journal Ecclesiastical History* 27.4, 337-58.

Harris, A. (2003), *Byzantium Britain & the West*, Tempus, Stroud.

Hawkins, A.B. (1973), 'Sea-level changes around south-west England', in Blackman (ed.) (1973), 67-87.

Heyworth, A. and Kidson, C. (1982), 'Sea-level changes in south-west England and Wales', *Proceedings of the Geological Association* 93.1, 91-111.

Hill, D. (1981), *An Atlas of Anglo-Saxon England*, Blackwell, Oxford.

Hillam, J., Groves, C.M., Brown, D.M., Baillie, M.G.L, Coles, J.M. and Coles, B.J. (1990), 'Dendrochronology of the English Neolithic', *Antiquity* 64.243, 210-20.

Hollinrake, C. and Hollinrake, N. (1992), 'The abbey enclosure ditch and a late-Saxon canal: rescue excavations at Glastonbury, 1984–1988', *Somerset Archaeology and Natural History* 136, 73-94.

Housley, R.A. (1988), 'The environmental context of Glastonbury Lake Village', *Somerset Levels Papers* 14, 63-82.

Keil, I. (1959-60), 'The garden at Glastonbury Abbey', *Proceedings of the Somerset Archaeological and Natural History Society* 104, 96-101.

Kelting, E.L. (1968), 'The Rivers and Sea-walls of Somerset', *Somerset Archaeology and Natural History* 12, 12-20.

Kenawell, W.W. (1965), *The Quest at Glastonbury. A biographical study of Frederick Bligh Bond*, Helix Press, New York.

Kent, O. 'Ceramic finds from archaeological excavations at Glastonbury Abbey, 1901-1979', *Somerset Archaeology and Natural History* 140, 73-104.

Keynes, S. (1994), 'The 'Dunstan-B' charters', *Anglo-Saxon England* 23, 165-193.

Krochalis, J. (1997), 'Magna tabula: the Glastonbury tablets', *Arthurian Literature* 15, 93-183.

Leach, P. and Ellis, P. (1993), 'The medieval precinct of Glastonbury Abbey' in Carver, 1993, 119-124.

Leach, P. (2001) *Excavations at Fosse Lane Shepton Mallet* Brittania Monograph Series No 18 Society for the Promotion of Roman Studies, London.

Leach, P. (2002) *Roman Somerset* Dovecote Press Dorset.

Lewis, A. (1997), 'Stained glass from Glastonbury', *Somerset Archaeology and Natural History* 140, 61-67.

Luxford, J.M. (2001), 'The great rood of Glastonbury Abbey', *Somerset Archaeology and Natural History* 145, 83-87.

Mitchener, M. (1986), *Medieval Pilgrim and Secular Badges*, Hawkin Publications, London.

Minnitt, S. and Coles, J. (1996), *The lake villages of Somerset*, Glastonbury Antiquarian Society, Glastonbury.

Morland, S.C. (1970), 'Hidation on the Glastonbury Estates', *Somerset Archaeology and Natural History* 114, 74-90.

Morland, S.C. (1984), 'Glaston Twelve Hides', *Somerset Archaeology and Natural History* 128, 35-54.

Morland, S.C. (1986), 'The Glastonbury Manors and their Charters', *Somerset Archaeology and Natural History* 130, 61-105.

Morris, J. (1973), *The Age of Arthur*, Weidenfeld and Nicolson, London.

Morris, R (1989), *Churches in the Landscape,* Dent.

Pevsner, N. (1958), *South and West Somerset (The Buildings of England)*, Penguin, London.

Radford, C.A.R (1962), 'The Church in Somerset down to 1100', *Proceedings of the Somerset Archaeological and Natural History Society* 106, 28-45.

Radford, C.A.R (1981), 'Glastonbury Abbey before 1184: interim report on the excavations, 1908-64' in *Medieval Art and Architecture at Wells and Glastonbury*, British Archaeological Association, Leeds, 110-34.

Radford, C.A.R and Swanton, M.J. (1975), *Arthurian Sites in the West*, Exeter University, Exeter.

Rahtz, P. (1964), 'Excavations at Chalice Well, Glastonbury', *Proceedings of the Somerset Archaeological and Natural History Society* 108, 143-63.

Rahtz, P. (1971), 'Excavations on Glastonbury Tor, Somerset, 1964-6', *Archaeological Journal* 127, 18l.

Rahtz, P. (1982), 'Celtic Society in Somerset A.D. 400-700', *Bulletin of the Board of Celtic Studies* 30, 176-200.

Rahtz, P. (1991), 'Pagan and Christian by the Severn Sea', in Abrams and Carley (eds.) (1991), 3-37.

Rahtz, P. (2002), 'Glastonbury Tor: a modified landscape', *Landscapes* 3, 4-18.

Rahtz, P. and Fowler, P.J. (1972), 'Somerset A.D. 400-700', in Fowler (ed.) (1972), 187-217.

Rahtz, P, and Hirst, S.M. (1974), Beckery Chapel, Glastonbury, 1967-8, Glastonbury Antiquarian Society, Glastonbury.

Rahtz, P. and Watts, L. (1979), 'The end of Roman temples in the west of Britain', in Casey, J. (ed.) (1979), *The End of Roman Britain*, British Archaeological Report 71, Oxford, 183-210.

Rahtz, P. and Watts, L. (1991), 'Pagans Hill revisited', *Archaeological Journal* 146, 322-71.

Rahtz, P., Hirst, S.M. and Wright, S.M. (2000), *Cannington Cemetery*, Society for the Promotion of Roman Studies, London.

Rippon, S. (1997), *The Severn Estuary: landscape evolution and wetland reclamation*, Leicester University Press, London.

Robinson, J.A. (1921), 'The Saxon Abbots of Glastonbury', *Somerset Historical Essays,* London, 26-53.

Robinson, J.A. (1923a), 'On the Old Church at Glastonbury', *Somerset and Dorset Notes and Queries* 18, no. 44, 58-62.

Robinson, J.A. (1923b). *The Times of St Dunstan*, Oxford (reprinted 1969).

Robinson, J.A. (1926), *Two Glastonbury Legends: King Arthur and Joseph of Arimathea*, Cambridge University Press, Cambridge.

Robinson, J.A. (1927), 'The historical evidence as to the Saxon church at Glastonbury', *Proceedings of the Somerset Archaeological and Natural History Society* 73, 40-49.

Robinson, J.L. (1953-4), 'St Brigid at Glastonbury', *Journal of the Royal Society of Ireland* 83.4, 97-9.

Scott, J. (1981), *The Early History of Glastonbury* (an edition, translation and study of William of Malmesbury's *De Antiquitate Glastonie Ecclesie*, Boydell Press, Woodbridge.

Stacy, N.E. (1999), 'Henry of Blois and the lordship of Glastonbury', *English Historical Review* 114, 1-33.

Stacy, N.E. (2001), *Surveys of the estates of Glastonbury Abbey*, Oxford University Press, Oxford, for the British Academy.

Thomas, C. (1971), *The Early Christian Archaeology of North Britain*, Oxford University Press, Oxford.

Thomas, C. (1981), *Christianity in Roman Britain to AD 500*, Batsford, London.

Thurlby, M. (1995), 'The Lady Chapel of Glastonbury Abbey', *Antiquaries' Journal* 75, 107-170.

Warner, R. (1826), *History of the Abbey of Glastobury and the Town of Glastonbury*, Richard Critwell, Bath.

Watkin, A. (1948-9), 'The earliest Glastonbury Seal' *Proceedings of the Somerset Archaeological Natural History Society* 94, 158-9.

Watkin, A. (1997), 'The Glastonbury legends', *Arthurian Literature* 15, 77-91.

Webster, C.J. (ed.) (2000), *Somerset archaeology: papers to mark 150 years of the Somerset Archaeological and Natural History Society*, Somerset County Council, Taunton.

Watts, D. (1991), *Christians and Pagans in Roman Britain*, Routledge, London.

Watts, D. (1998), *Religion in Late Roman Britain*, Routledge, London.

Williams, M. (1970), *The Drainage of the Somerset Levels*, Cambridge University Press, Cambridge

Willis, R. (1866), *Architectural History of Glastonbury Abbey*, Cambridge.

Wilson, D. (ed.) (1976), *The Archaeology of Anglo-Saxon England*, Methuen, London.

Woods, H. (1994), 'Excavations at Glastonbury Abbey, 1987-1993', *Somerset Archaeology and Natural History Society* 138, 7-73.

Woodward, A. (1992), *Shrines and Sacrifice*, Batsford/English Heritage, London.

The Victoria County History for Glastonbury has recently been completed by Robert Dunning and Mary Siraut. Volume 9 was published in 2006.

GLOSSARY

Celtic

Strictly speaking refers only to language, but commonly used for all aspects of indigenous pre-English society in Britain, such as art or the Church.

censer

A covered perforated metal container to hold burning incense; usually attached to a chain, by which it could be swung to disperse the perfume.

charter

A document conferring or confirming the possession of, or rights in, land or other property.

chevron moulding

Zig-zag ornament on architecture of the Norman period.

coppicing

Technique of growing and managing trees, so that they can be repeatedly trimmed to provide light timbers for fencing, hurdling or other purposes.

crannog

An artificial island in a lake, on which a settlement was built: such constructions date from prehistoric times to as recently as the seventeenth century.

daughter-house

Monastic foundation in a new place, set up by monks or nuns from an established monastery.

dendrochronology

Method for dating timbers from the pattern of the growth rings of the trees from which they were made.

dorter

Building or upper room in an abbey used for sleeping (as dormitory).

epigraphic evidence

Information from inscriptions cut in wood, stone or other material.

escutcheon

Decorative emblem of an aristocratic family, such as used on burial monuments.

ferrule
Pointed metal end piece fixed on rod or stick.

Grail
Holy vessel associated with the Last Supper and Passion of Christ; it became a powerful symbol in Arthurian mythology.

Gregorian chant
A form of music used in churches and monasteries in the early history of the Church.

historiography
The history of a particular field of study.

henges
Circular monuments of earth and timber or stone, of the Neolithic period; used for religious and other communal events.

interpolation
Part of a text that had been added by a later writer, and thus cannot be relied upon.

ley-lines
Proposed paths of force between ritual centres.

***Lives* (of saints)**
Biographies of holy men or women; they are likely to be idealised rather than true accounts.

Mesolithic
Middle Stone Age, c.10,000-5,000 BC, but overlapping with Palaeolithic and Neolithic; characterised by finely worked stone tools, and an economy based principally on hunting and food-gathering.

millefiori
Technique of drawing out composite coloured glass rods and cutting slices from them, for setting in metal or enamel.

Neolithic
New Stone Age, c.5000-2000 BC; characterised by the first use of polished stone tools, pottery, impressive ritual centres and permanent settlements.

Palaeolithic
Old Stone Age, from earliest emergence of human beings to c.10,000 BC.

Passion
The suffering and death of Christ.

post-hole
Hole dug to provide a firm base for upright post, usually in building; often with stone packing.

radiocarbon dating

Method for dating organic substances by the measurement of surviving radiocarbon, which decreases with age at a steady rate.

ridge and furrow

Technique of preparing ground for arable cultivation into long narrow raised strips, separated by ditches; characteristic of the medieval period and still very visible in many parts of Britain.

Romanesque

Style of art and architecture characteristic of the eleventh/twelfth centuries in Europe.

stake-hole

Hole made by driving a pointed timber into the ground.

stratigraphy

The study of stratification: the layers which comprise an archaeological sequence.

seal

A wax patch attached to a document to ensure its authenticity; the seal carries the impression of a metal die, with insignia of the confirming authority.

tessera

Roughly-shaped small coloured cube of stone or other material, used as the unit for mosaic work.

timber-slot

A rectilinear shallow trench cut in the ground, in which is bedded a horizontal foundation timber of a building.

Tor Burrs

Boulders of harder stone within the Midford Sand capping of Glastonbury Tor; many have become detached by erosion and have tumbled down the slopes.

translation (of body)

The removal of the physical remains of a holy person from one place to another, often from a grave to a shrine; an event accompanied by ceremony.

triforium

The arches above the main arcade, usually with a passage behind them; often surmounted by an upper stage, with windows.

tympanum

Semicircular stone slab set in arch of doorway, often decorated with symbols or figures.

urn

Vessel of metal or pottery, used for the deposition of cremated human bone and associated finds.

INDEX

(Numbers in **bold** refer to illustrations)